Las Vegas

Front cover: Lights of the Las Vegas Strip

Right: Vegas Vic – a neon star of the
Fremont Street Experience

TOP 10 ATTRACTIONS

The Big Shot at the Stratosphere • A must for thrill seekers *(page 43)*

Bellagio • The spectacular fountains in front of this lavish casino-resort make it an unmissable attraction *(page 35)*

The Fremont Street Experience •
With over 2 million lights, it's neon nirvana *(page 45)*

The Guggenheim Hermitage • This classy museum has a great collection of art, including pieces by world-famous artists *(page 59)*

The Luxor • This resort is housed in a huge pyramid *(page 29)*

Hoover Dam • A marvel of 1930s engineering *(page 61)*

Wynn Las Vegas • Sleek and ultra luxurious, this is the ultimate Vegas resort *(page 41)*

Miracle Mile • A unique retail-therapy experience, complete with an indoor waterfall *(page 34)*

Binion's Gambling Hall • Downtown casinos offer the best value, and this place is among the best *(page 49)*

The Grand Canyon • One of the wonders of the natural world, and just an excursion away from Vegas *(page 66)*

CONTENTS

26

80

9

Features

INTRODUCTION

Only 100 years ago, this city of mythic proportion and impossible illusion was no more than a dusty railroad stop in the middle of an unforgiving desert valley. Dramatic changes occurred in the valley throughout the 20th century to create this fantasy, known today as the 'Entertainment Capital of the World.'

Initially settled in the mid 1800s, Las Vegas struggled as an isolated outpost for much of its early existence. The site was only declared a town in 1905. That year, on May 15, officials from the San Pedro, Los Angeles & Salt Lake Railroad auctioned 1,200 parcels of land mapping 40 square blocks in the desert dust. Within a year, the city's population had grown to 1,500 brave pioneers.

Landmarks of the Modern World

Today's visitors are greeted by the fastest-growing, most rapidly changing city in the American West. They mingle and play among iconic landmarks of the world's great cities. Replicas of the Eiffel Tower, the skyscrapers of Manhattan, the palaces of ancient Rome, and an Egyptian pyramid loom to entrance and entice.

Modern visitors see very little trace of the features that spawned and nurtured the fledgling city – its natural springs – most of which have long since run dry. Though water flows freely through the artificial lakes, lush resort swimming areas, and sprinklers for the famous golf courses, it now comes in a giant pipeline from the Colorado River. Without that pipeline, the city would dry up and crumble back into the desert.

The Las Vegas Strip

Fast Lane

Las Vegas is located in Clark County, Nevada, near the southern tip of the state. Clark County has about 1.9 million inhabitants, and over 95 percent of them reside in metropolitan Las Vegas. Nevada, which ranks as the seventh largest state in the union by area, has a total of just 2.5 million inhabitants, making it only the 35th most populous state. The population of retired people is growing four times as fast as in the rest of the United States, and for four decades in a row Nevada has been the fastest-growing state in America.

Sunny Days

Las Vegas has an average of just four inches (10cm) of rainfall and 310 days of sunshine each year. Summers are hot, with temperatures often nearing 115°F (46°C). In winter, daytime temperatures can be a pleasant 65°F (18°C), but nights are cold. Early spring and late fall are the best times to visit, as the days are warm and the nights comfortably cool.

Rush to the New

Las Vegas is unfettered by the burdens of history or preservation. Old buildings or resorts simply give way to the pres-

World Capital of Boxing

Las Vegas probably has a better claim than any city to the title of 'the World's Capital of Boxing.' Vegas is often the promoters' choice as the venue for major title bouts, including world championships.

Sonny Liston, Muhammad Ali, Leon Spinks, Larry Holmes, Mike Spinks, George Foreman, and Evander Holyfield are just a few of the fighters to have won the heavyweight championship title in Las Vegas. After his retirement from the ring, Joe Louis stayed on and was popular as a greeter at Caesars Palace.

sures of age or fashion and are remodeled, or, at the extreme, imploded, accompanied by fireworks and street-wide celebration. Few remember, or perhaps even care, that the Italian-themed Venetian is on the site of the Sands – the Rat Pack's most famous haunt.

Las Vegas, like a gambler, has often reinvented itself. After the Mob era, Sin City became a family-friendly destination, building theme parks and spectacular attractions with children in mind. This was a success throughout the 1990s, but the turn of the millennium brought a sea change. Families, it turns out, spend less

The fuel that builds and runs all of Las Vegas

time at the all-important gaming tables than do singles or couples. Although kid friendly places like Excalibur still market to families, the emphasis has shifted to lure in as many high-spending adults as possible. Today's Las Vegas has world-class accommodations, five-star dining, and shopping that rivals any major city, added to the town's reputation for all-night gambling, drinking, and adult-oriented diversions. Hotel-casinos have positioned themselves as complete resorts, offering day spas, spectacular productions and huge shopping malls – in addition to the gambling, golf courses, and showrooms, of course. Newer resorts, like Bellagio and Wynn Las Vegas, aim to recap-

New York-New York; it's one heck of a sight

ture the perceived glamour of the Rat Pack era. Always betting on growth, expansion, and the power of positive cash flow, Las Vegas has transformed itself twice in 10 years. Today, the north end of the Strip is undergoing yet another transformation, with the construction of huge multiple-use condo-hotel complexes such as the Trump Towers, Echelon and City Center.

Reinvention
Such rapid change and reinvention results in what many call a city without a soul. But for nearly 500,000 residents and 30 million annual visitors, this characteristic – the city's instinct for the next big thing – makes Vegas the city of their dreams. In fact, many come as visitors and choose to stay. About 5,000 become new residents each month, pushing the population of the valley up by more than 1,200 percent since that first railroad auction.

Outside the resort corridors, new suburban residential developments swallow the surrounding desert, edging to the bases of the mountain ranges east and west. Unlike the original American suburbs, new master-planned communities like Summerlin and Green Valley are thriving cities within themselves. New businesses spring up almost immediately, built into the plan and ready to serve an already-waiting community of clients. Driving through these areas feels like a ride through a movie set – the homes are sparkling and modern, the highways smooth and wide, and the landscaping young, fragile, and new.

Local Las Vegas

Just a short way from the crowds and lights of Fremont Street and Glitter Gulch, are quiet, ranch-style homes complete with swimming pools, tennis courts, horse corrals, and lush landscaping. The University of Nevada-Las Vegas mentors a student population of over 28,000, although, like most people in Vegas, they are commuters through the endless gridlock that now defines the streets. Before the recent rapid expansion, the city claimed to have more churches per capita than any other in the United States. Spiritual guidance was apparently a pressing need for the dwellers on the excessive fringes of temptation.

Live jazz at the Gold Coast Hotel and Casino

Although Las Vegas is still dominated by the gambling industry, non-gaming business flourishes here as well, thanks to the county's and state's favorable tax structure. Much of the non-gaming business is in suburban business parks and master-planned communities, an effort to reinvent the metropolis with industrial and commercial centers across the valley. Credit-card companies and banks, mail order firms, health care subsidiaries, and software developers are all in the economic mix. They help Las Vegas to diversify, as the national attitudes to gambling shift like the desert sands.

Las Vegas shows new cultural growth, too. Local theater is healthy, while a well-regarded public art museum and the Guggenheim Hermitage Museum have both brought world-class art collections to an eager public.

Spectacular Sports

For athletic visitors, and locals, too, one of the attractions of this city in the desert is its easy access to sports. Whether you watch from a ring-side seat as great events unfold, like Oscar de la Hoya winning a championship fight or auto-racer Jimmie Johnson roaring past the checkered flag at the Las Vegas Motor Speedway, or take active advantage of the golf, hot-air ballooning, tennis, hiking, or canoeing possibilities, nothing is ever far away. Nor are some of the most important wonders of the world, whether they be natural – like the Grand Canyon and Death Valley – or man-made, like the very impressive Hoover Dam.

Las Vegas' shows – musical, magical, or just totally theatrical – are among the

Get hitched in the shadow of the Stratosphere Tower

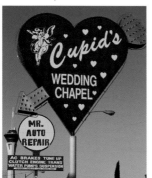

The fabulous Wynn Las Vegas resort

best in the world, employing the finest of Hollywood muscle to build state-of-the-art performance arenas that encourage extravaganzas to reach new heights. And while Sin City confronts the same issues that face all growing cities – crime, the problems of growth and expansion – Las Vegas continues to amply demonstrate just what a 21st-century megalopolis can accomplish.

Glittering Moments

Las Vegas's transformations – from a watering hole, via a gambling way-station to a desert retreat for Hollywood heavyweights, and now, to an international resort city – have all been whistle-stops on the city's journey of evolution. This city, with its eyes always firmly on the future, is never dull, and it continues to attract tourists in their millions who want to sample the glamorous Las Vegas lifestyle, if only for a few non-stop moments.

A BRIEF HISTORY

The inhabited history of the Las Vegas Valley has been traced to 23,000BC, when much of the area was covered by a prehistoric sea. The people of the time lived in caves, hunting mammals that gathered at the shoreline. The landscape of the valley changed dramatically over the next 200 centuries. The glaciers feeding the lake melted and the lake evaporated. Fossils tell a story of man's slow development.

First Inhabitants

Around 3000BC, native Archaic people began the development of a lasting hunter-gatherer culture. By this time, the valley was geographically similar to how it is today, with the exception of artesian springs bubbling to the surface. The springs fed a network of streams, draining through the Las Vegas Wash to the Colorado River. Surrounding the springs were desert oases, sprawls of grasses, trees, and wildlife. Many of the springs crossed the center of the modern Las Vegas metropolitan area.

For about 4,000 years, the Archaics, in a culture with many signs of early civilization. Further advancement appeared halfway through the first millennium AD, with the arrival of the Anasazi people. More progressive than the Archaics, the Anasazi used agricultural techniques like irrigation to nourish their crops. The Anasazi reached a benchmark of advanced society – living in permanent shelters year-round, without the need to follow wildlife. Mysteriously, the Anasazi vanished from the valley around AD1150, leaving it to be repopulated by

Fish in the desert

275 million years ago, the Mojave, Great Basin, and Sonoran deserts formed the floor of a great inland sea.

Petroglyphs in the Clark County Historical Museum

another hunter-gatherer tribe, the Southern Paiutes. Unskilled in the agri-techniques of the Anasazi, the Paiutes were semi-nomadic until European settlers arrived and changed the cultural landscape of the valley.

From Mailmen to Mormons

In the early 19th century, America's western territories were still largely unexplored. It was not until 1829 that Rafael Rivera, a Mexican scout, found a spring-fed valley and dubbed it '*Las Vegas*' – a Spanish name that leaves many modern visitors wondering exactly where 'the meadows' really are.

For 15 years, Las Vegas was used as a Spanish Trail way-station. In 1844, American explorer John C. Fremont parked his horses at Big Springs, and his report to the government resulted in a mail route leading past the spot on its way to California. This put Las Vegas on the map and was one of the crucial turning points of its history. In 1855, Mormon leader

Brigham Young responded to promising reports of this oasis by sending 30 missionary settlers to the valley; they eventually built a fort near today's downtown area. Surrounded by farmland hewn from the hard desert, this adobe fort was the center of Las Vegas' development for 50 years. The missionaries struggled valiantly against the harsh desert, trying to both survive in the terrain and spread the Mormon faith. But pressures from arriving miners pushed the missionaries' plight beyond recovery. Their supplies scarce, their harvest meager, and their spirit broken, they abandoned the fort in 1858.

Although the local land was rich in silver, by 1865 most of the mining traffic through Las Vegas was of prospectors headed to California or Northern Nevada in the quest for gold.

Explorer John C. Fremont

Las Vegas Ranch

One opportunist who stayed was Octavius Decatur Gass. Having plenty of the pioneer spirit that characterizes Las Vegas to this day, Gass picked up where the Mormons left off, with ranching and farming. He took over the abandoned fort and 640 acres (260 hectares) surrounding it, naming it the Las Vegas Ranch. He expanded the ranch and irrigated the land to support crops and cattle. Gass became a Justice of the Peace and a territorial legislator, but despite his ambition, his

success was short-lived. In
the late 1870s, he defaulted
on a loan from rancher
Archibald Stewart, and
Stewart took the Las Vegas
Ranch for his own. True to
Wild-West stereotypes, Stewart was slain by a neighbor-
ing farmer, leaving the ranch

Native legacy

Native Americans inhabited
the Las Vegas Valley for
about 5,000 years. First
came the so-called Archaics,
then, around 300BC the
Anasazi, and more recently
the Paiutes.

to his strong-willed wife, Helen. Through 1905, Helen Stewart expanded the ranch to 2,000 acres (810 hectares), making herself quite a bit of money in the process.

What happened next would mark the end of the successful Las Vegas Ranch and the beginning of the era of the sub-
division seen across almost all of western America to this
day. The railroad was coming, and when it arrived, Las Vegas
would never be the same again.

Of Tracks and Tracts

At the turn of the 19th century Los Angeles and Salt Lake
City were among the burgeoning metropolises of the new
American West. When the two cities were linked by rail, the
Las Vegas Valley (which at the time had a non-native popu-
lation of less than 30) changed again.

In 1903, officials of the San Pedro, Los Angeles and Salt
Lake Railroad arrived in Las Vegas, eager to secure a right-
of-way for their Los Angeles–Salt Lake connection. Las Vegas
would serve as a major stopover for crew rest and train repairs. For all this, the railroad needed land. As mapped, the
track traveled directly through Helen Stewart's Las Vegas
Ranch, so Stewart sold 99.5 percent of her ranch to the railroad. The remainder she returned to the native Paiutes.

The route between Los Angeles and Salt Lake City was
completed in 1905 and railroad tracks bore right into the

center of the Las Vegas Valley. On May 15, 1905, the railroad held a land sale – a milestone in Las Vegas history. Standing at the depot at Main and Fremont streets, officials auctioned 1,200 lots, subdivided from 40 square blocks of desert scrub. Land speculators and locals alike were anxious for a part of the newest railroad boomtown, and more than 80 percent of the lots were sold that afternoon.

Las Vegas was no longer a small pioneer settlement. With rail service in place and 40 blocks of private property, it was ready to become a real town. Businesses sprang up overnight, and wooden houses were erected to replace the tent city where many of the early settlers lived. One year after the auction, the population of Las Vegas had swelled to 1,500 residents.

Dam Good Luck

From the beginning, Las Vegas had served travelers, first on the Spanish or Paiute Trail, then the mail route. Now the railroad needed a way station, and Las Vegas was the place. By 1915, after 10 years of growth, the town had telephones, 24-hour electricity, and a growing population – many of whom worked in the railroad repair shop.

With growing competition in rail transport, Union Pacific bought the Los Angeles–Salt Lake line. Union Pacific then consolidated its operations, eliminating the Las Vegas repair facility. Las Vegas had been incorporated into Nevada's new Clark County in 1909, when the legislature also outlawed gambling. These circumstances threatened to relegate Las Vegas to the status of a small desert community struggling to support its 3,000 residents. But the Southwest's growing need for water, combined with

The first casino

Mayme Stocker, the wife of a railroad man, was granted the first Las Vegas gambling license. She opened The Northern Club on Fremont Street in 1920.

Las Vegas shortly after the construction of the Hoover Dam

fortuitous proximity to the Colorado River, would give Las Vegas a second chance of prosperity. Construction on the Hoover Dam (originally called the 'Boulder Dam,' and later renamed for the president who authorized it) began in 1931, in a canyon 45 miles (72km) southeast of Las Vegas.

Bringing $165 million to the southwestern economy, the Hoover Dam prevented Las Vegas from drying up, financially and literally. The project brought jobs and created Lake Mead, the massive reservoir that provides the water for the whole of southern Nevada.

Public Relations

The construction of the Hoover Dam wasn't Las Vegas' sole savior, however. The state legislature helped too, legalizing gambling in 1931 and securing the future of the town. The hordes of people who attended the dam's 1935 dedication set the city's now-formidable public relations machine into action. They went to work on what has become one of the lengthiest tourism campaigns ever attempted. The city soon established itself as a Wild-West town with an 'anything goes' attitude. Vices outlawed or heavily controlled elsewhere were legal here, at any hour of any day or night. So began Las Vegas's reputation as an adult theme park.

Further fuel for the valley's economy came with World War II. The Las Vegas Aerial Gunnery School, now Nellis Air Force Base and the Nevada Test Site, in the north, and Basic Magnesium in nearby Henderson, grew from America's war effort. By 1945, the population had grown to almost 20,000, with workers and airmen moving in at a pace.

Gambling and the Rat Pack

Gaming thrived Downtown in the 1930s and early 1940s, and casinos emerged on the stretch of the old Los Angeles Highway now known as the Strip; El Rancho Vegas was the first, in 1941. Then a new migrant came onto the Strip – the

The Mob in Vegas

In 1946, Benjamin 'Bugsy' Siegel opened the Flamingo, an opulent resort on the southern end of the LA Highway. His vision was Hollywood flair, the new Vegas flash with Mob money. But the Mafia bosses weren't pleased with its performance and Siegel was murdered in the summer of 1947. Despite its initial failings, Siegel's Flamingo survived him, as did Mob infiltration of casinos.

Money from the Teamsters Union was used to fund the Stardust and other casino operations; the unions' total investment in Las Vegas was shown to exceed $238 million. Law enforcement investigations, beginning with the hearings of Tennessee Senator Estes Kefauver in 1950, took until the late 1960s to make a serious impact on the influence of organized crime in the Las Vegas gaming business.

Robbie the robot takes to the tables, 1957

Mob *(see page 20)*. From the mid-1940s to the mid-1960s, emerging stars came to Las Vegas with dreams of making it big: Frank Sinatra, Wayne Newton, and Louis Prima among them. The Rat Pack – originally Frank Sinatra, Dean Martin, Sammy Davis Jr, Peter Lawford, and Joey Bishop, made legendary appearances at the Sands in January 1960, including filming the original *Ocean's 11*. To capitalize on the increasing popularity, more casinos emerged along the Strip, including the Desert Inn, Sahara, Sands, and Riviera.

New Legitimacy

In the 1960s, organized crime met a formidable rival for control of Las Vegas – corporate cash. First came the arrival in 1966 of billionaire Howard Hughes. As a recluse and an invalid, Hughes was borne on a stretcher to the Desert Inn's penthouse. Six weeks later he was asked – then instructed – to vacate the suite for the high rollers who had previously booked it. Hughes immediately bought the Desert Inn and fired the management. During his three-year residence, he never once allowed cleaners into the suite, and he saw no-one face to face except for his bodyguards. Yet Hughes' $300-million Las Vegas buying spree took in many properties along the Strip, plus plots of land from the Strip to the mountains.

Hughes' influence would have beneficial repercussions, both immediate and lasting. Because of the legitimacy Hughes conferred by investments, established companies such as Hilton Hotels bought into the gaming business, and their influence drew a line in the desert sand between lawful operations and Mob casinos, where illegal skimming of profits was rife. That, and the formation of the Nevada Gaming Control Board, helped turn the tide against Mob influence in the city.

Las Vegas with a Vision

The legitimization of gambling led to disorganization and reassessment. The competition forced casino operators to look again at their business models and their markets. Leading the way was Steve Wynn, a Vegas resident and owner of the Golden Nugget casino. In the mid-1980s, Wynn began to reinvigorate the Strip.

He bought several key properties – the Silver Slipper and Castaways among them – and demolished them to make way for a new kind of resort. The Mirage was an instant success. Wynn's demolition of existing properties started a trend that led to many more implosions. The Dunes was replaced by Bel-

Collecting casinos

Howard Hughes stayed in Las Vegas for almost exactly three years. In that time he bought the Desert Inn, Landmark, Frontier, Silver Slipper, and Sands casinos, three more parcels of land on the Strip, an airline, and a TV station. According to legend he bought the TV station just so he could choose the late-night films that they aired.

Elvis and Priscilla at their Vegas wedding in 1967

lagio, Aladdin by the new Aladdin, and the Sands made way for the Venetian. Wynn's casinos have also set new standards of fantasy – Excalibur, the MGM Grand, the Luxor, and New York-New York all followed Mirage's lead during the 1990s, offering themed environments and family attractions.

The Modern Era

By the middle of the 1990s, the new approach brought a backlash; visitors found the Las Vegas experience was becoming mediocre. In response, new resorts started to offer attractions and amenities modeled after top worldwide resorts, including spas and fabulous swimming pools, signature restaurants and exclusive boutiques.

Some of these resorts – such as Wynn Las Vegas, Mandalay Bay, Paris Las Vegas, the Venetian, Bellagio and the Four Seasons – now market themselves squarely at the luxury travel market. Guests at these resorts expect, and receive the best; the most basic of amenities includes five-star dining, personal attention and world-class art exhibitions. These high-end accommodations with their glittering clientele have raised expectations far above even the glamorous mythology of the Rat Pack era.

City of the Future

As it changed from Mob gambling town to corporate gaming venue, the population of Las Vegas skyrocketed. Over 20,000 additional hotel rooms have been added in a few short years, including resorts in Summerlin and Lake Las Vegas. Most of the remaining Rat-Pack-era Strip hotels have already been demolished to make way for big condominium projects. Recent projections for Las Vegas predict challenges; revenues need to rise continually to sustain the investments, and a shortage of power – essential to air condition and spotlight this neon nirvana in the desert – is an on-going concern.

A vision of the modern city is Paris Las Vegas

Still, the future is sure to be in the pioneering spirit that built the city from a few springs in the desert to the fantasy that it is today. With its image constantly repositioning, its good looks glittering, and its careful aim in sight, Las Vegas seems worth a pretty hefty wager.

Historical Landmarks

1150 Paiute Indians inhabit Las Vegas Valley, replacing the Anasazi.

1829 Scout Raphael Rivera discovers springs in the desert and names the land 'Las Vegas,' which is Spanish for 'the meadows.'

1844 Explorer John C. Fremont camps at Las Vegas Springs, on a site that later bears his name, Fremont Street.

1848 The US acquires the region after winning the Mexican War.

1855 Mormon settlers build an adobe fort to protect the mail route.

1905 The San Pedro, Los Angeles & Salt Lake Railroad makes an inaugural run and auctions lots in a new town called Las Vegas.

1931 Construction of the Hoover Dam commences.

1931 Gambling is legalized in Nevada.

1941 El Rancho Vegas is the first casino to open on the stretch of Los Angeles Highway that later became known as the Strip.

1946 Benjamin 'Bugsy' Siegel, a member of the Meyer Lansky crime organization, opens the Flamingo Hotel.

1960 The Rat Pack shows, with Frank Sinatra, Sammy Davis Jr, Dean Martin, Peter Lawford, and Joey Bishop, sell out the Sands.

1966 Howard Hughes' arrival at the Desert Inn heralds the new corporate era of Las Vegas gaming.

1975 Nevada gaming revenues top $1 billion.

1980 Las Vegas (population 164,674) celebrates its 75th birthday.

1989 Steve Wynn opens the Mirage casino with 3,039 rooms.

1994 Work begins Downtown on the Fremont Street Experience.

1995 The Fremont Street Experience opens. A monorail connects the MGM Grand and Bally's.

1999 Mandalay Bay, New York-New York, and Paris Las Vegas open.

2001 The famous Desert Inn is imploded.

2004 Monorail extension runs the length of the Strip.

2005 The luxurious Wynn Las Vegas opens on the Strip.

2006 The Aladdin resort rebrands itself as Planet Hollywood.

2007 The Stardust and the New Frontier are demolished. The metropolitan population approaches 2 million.

WHERE TO GO

Since Bugsy Siegel's Flamingo Hotel set a new standard in 1946, nothing in the world could rival the Las Vegas Strip's audacity or the casinos' desire to outdo each other. This 3½-mile (5.5-km) section of the old Los Angeles Highway is both famous and notorious for its extravagant recreation. Stretching from the Mandalay Bay resort in the south to the Stratosphere Tower to the north, this one road has evoked more melodrama and mythology than the rest of the city combined.

Miles of neon tubing and millions of dazzling incandescent and fiber optic lights illuminate every hour of darkness year-round, while casinos that never close leave the doors to their comfortably air-conditioned interiors wide open, even while the summer sun burns down at 115°F (46°C). The excess is staggering, but visitors come to play and partake from all the far corners of the world.

Glittering Playground

A cornucopia of resorts, stores, restaurants, and – of course – glittering casinos line both sides of the thoroughfare, tantalizing onlookers. Dozens of the world's largest hotels are congregated directly around the action, simply because the hotels *are* the major attractions. Some of these mega-resorts revel in the clichés of the past, while others offer a chic opulence that borders on the unreal. Roman palaces, the Eiffel Tower, the pyramids of Egypt, and the jungles of Polynesia all await anyone with a yen to indulge in the extravagance, and a bankroll to withstand the trip.

The Venetian *(see page 39)*

Optical illusions

Las Vegas may be the only place on earth where architects work to make buildings seem smaller than they are.

THE STRIP – SOUTH

At the southernmost end of the glittering, never-ending Strip is the **Mandalay Bay Resort and Casino**. The $950-million behemoth has a South Seas theme and a unique 'hotel-with-in-a-hotel': opulent rooms managed by the Four Seasons group *(see below)*. Central to Mandalay's jungle-city theme is an 11-acre (4.5-hectare) tropical environment, complete with a wave pool that beats upon a sandy beach. Also featured are a House of Blues restaurant and club, a 12,000-seat arena, a convention center, and a spa. Mandalay's excellent restaurants include Aureole, China Grill, Wolfgang Puck's Trattoria del Lupo, and a great vodka bar.

The Four Seasons company, renowned for its superlative attention to guests' needs (poor customer service is a major complaint at most Las Vegas resorts), offers one of Las Vegas's only non-gaming resorts within the Mandalay Bay, the **Four Seasons Hotel Las Vegas**. A total of 424 ultra-luxury rooms and suites occupy floors 35 to 39 of the Mandalay Bay tower, reachable only via a private elevator in the Four Seasons' lobby. A separate driveway leads to a two-story main building housing four restaurants and bars, a health spa, and meeting rooms. A huge pool set in a lush garden is available only to hotel guests. If your priorities are for comfort first and gambling second, the Four Seasons Hotel is for you.

Next up along the Strip is the mighty black peak of the

Lost civilization

It's not easy to tone down the ancient-Egyptian theme in a hotel shaped like a giant pyramid, but that's exactly what the Luxor plans to do. The resort has declared itself Art Deco (a style that incorporates some Egyptian elements). The bazaar-themed shopping area has been supplanted by chic clubs and restaurants, and the guest rooms will be redecorated in 2009.

The Luxor's spectacular Sphinx

Luxor Hotel and Casino, 30 stories of tinted glass and steel topped with a night-defiant shaft of light, visible by air from Los Angeles (they say). Encompassing the world's largest atrium, the pyramid (and its two adjoining towers) house over 4,400 rooms and a stunningly huge casino. There are other attractions worth noting, though, including the Nurture Spa, and the LAX nightclub. One of the biggest thrills for guests of the hotel is the ride to the bedroom on the 'inclinator,' an elevator that moves up and sideways at the same time.

Excalibur

One of the first resorts with a theme, the **Excalibur Hotel and Casino** is a Medieval Faire aimed squarely at families and travelers on a budget. This is evident in the execution – though in no way shoddy, the overall experience is cheap and cheerful. For a brief period, the Excalibur was the largest hotel in the world, though its 4,008 rooms were

Medieval fantasy at Excalibur

soon surpassed by the MGM Grand. One of its attractions is the rowdy *Tournament of Kings*, a re-creation in a showroom of a Middle Ages jousting tournament, and one of the few dinner shows left in Las Vegas. The 100,000-sq-ft (9,300-sq-m) casino caters mostly to minimum betters, with $3 blackjack tables and nickel and dime slot machines. The resort, like most of Las Vegas, is definitely seen at its best in the nighttime – viewed from the Strip, the brightly illuminated spires and battlements are a fine sight.

Tropicana

The smallest and oldest of the four resorts at the busy intersection of Las Vegas Boulevard and Tropicana Avenue, the **Tropicana Resort and Casino** ignored the family-aimed marketing of the 1990s and held pretty tightly to the notion of Las Vegas as an adult escape. The main showroom's *Folies Bergères* has wooed audiences with its topless showgirls since 1961. The understated class of the hotel tower may have lost some luster but still retains an air of respectability, while the tropical pool area (with swim-up blackjack tables) is nearly perfect. Long-term attractions include the *Titanic Artifact Exhibit* and *Bodies – The Exhibition* (both open 10am–11pm).

MGM Grand

Across the Strip, the MGM **Grand Hotel and Casino** is so massive – the casino floor is the size of four American football fields – that most visitors become completely disoriented as they wander the resort. Past guests may remember the overly cute Wizard of Oz theme, which has been replaced in a multi-million-dollar renovation by a more mature style incorporating MGM's most famous movies. How big is big? Try 5,034 guest rooms spread across 114 acres (46 hectares), 22 places to eat (including establishments by Wolfgang Puck, Emeril Lagasse, and Mark Miller), an elaborate 6½-acre (3-hectare) pool complex, a spa and tennis facility, three arenas, including the enormous Grand Garden – site of some of Vegas' biggest rock concerts – a comedy club, and the Studio 54 nightclub. There are four gaming areas, each with a different theme, and minimum bets ranging from $5 to $500, as well as nearly 4,000 slot machines and lively sports betting. High rollers may be offered accommodations in one of 30 private villas at The Mansion. Like most casinos, the MGM Grand now operates loyalty-card-style schemes for players to accumulate perks, known locally as 'comps.'

The MGM Grand

New York-New York

Taking theme hotels to a new level, the **New York-New York Hotel and Casino** actually spawned lawsuits by Manhattan architects. Its dozen towers are uncanny, one-third-size replicas of famous New York skyscrapers, including the Empire State

Slot machines in New York-New York

Building, the New York Public Library, and the Chrysler Building. Inside, the detailed illusion continues with cartoon quality, such as the fake subway station complete with graffiti, Coney Island arcade, and 84,000-sq-ft (7,812-sq-m) casino area fashioned after Central Park – right down to the trees, footbridges, and street lamps. Guestrooms have names like Park Avenue Deluxe, while shopping areas are called Soho Village and Grand Central. The Big Apple Bar is open 24 hours a day, and the **Manhattan Express roller coaster** is worth the wait.

Monte Carlo

The **Monte Carlo Hotel and Casino** evokes a classic Las Vegas atmosphere, remarkably accessible to any traveler. Striking in its elegant European theme, this resort has an understated style rare in modern Las Vegas. In homage to tradition, the resort offers a wide range of gaming, dining, retail, and spa amenities. Though it looks like a haven for high rollers, minimum bets are actually quite modest, starting at $5; they even have 5¢ slots. The **Lance Burton Theatre** showcases the entertaining and amusing act of this classic Las Vegas performer, who has been bewildering audiences with his magic tricks since 1991.

Planet Hollywood

Across the street is the **Planet Hollywood Hotel and Casino,** formerly the Aladdin. The original 1960s Aladdin played host to the 1967 wedding of Elvis and Priscilla Presley. It was reopened in 1976 after a total renovation and was owned for a time by Vegas legend Wayne Newton. The hotel was imploded in 1998, and a new 21st-century version was opened in August 2000. Despite spacious bedrooms upstairs for its resident guests and a beautiful casino with murals and soft lighting, the resort teetered on the brink of bankruptcy. In 2007, the Aladdin re-emerged as the resort of Planet Hollywood, complete with celebrity-inspired decor. Floor-to-

Slot Machines

Slot machines generate two-thirds of Nevada casinos' take, with the nickel slots producing $1 billion annually. Today, slots take up 60 percent of casino floor space and generate more profits for the casinos than from all table games combined. Currently, casinos average about 3,000 slots apiece. The programming of the machines makes a jackpot rare enough for the big pay off, but still allows for a tidy profit for the casino. Most machines are set to pay out somewhere between 83 and 98 percent, but slot payoffs vary from one casino to another.

The phenomenal popularity of slot machines may be because they require no skill, and the pace can be set by the player. Players are driven by the idea that a machine will be ready to pay off after a certain amount of play, though payouts are more likely to be random.

ceiling Swarovski crystal chandeliers adorn the lobby, while the swimming pool and spa overlook the Strip.

Adjoining the resort is the spectacular **Miracle Mile** shopping promenade, with a distinctive array of 170 stores and an indoor waterfall. The miles of shopping aisles are gradually being transformed from their original Moorish theme to an ultramodern look.

Paris Las Vegas

The **Paris Las Vegas Hotel and Casino** took the theme concept to new levels with this massive $750-million, 2,900-room hotel-casino, modeled after the Hôtel de Ville in Paris. The property is a Vegas-style homage to the city of romance, complete with Arc de Triomphe. Patrons can see the bright city lights from the top of the one-half scale Eiffel Tower, go shopping on the Rue de la Paix, or dine in one of eight

Paris Las Vegas

Parisian-inspired eateries, including a restaurant in the tower itself. Cobblestone walkways lead to other landmark replicas, among them the Paris Opera House and the Louvre. After 11pm, you can even arrange for a wedding ceremony at the top of the tower. Be prepared for high minimum stakes in the gilded casino, however, where gaming opportunities include more than 2,000 slot machines.

Ooh la la!

One of the old guard of Las Vegas resorts, **Bally's Hotel and Casino** has eschewed transformation over the years. Despite the $14 million futuristic light-and-water show out front, Bally's is an exercise in classic Las Vegas style. Inside, all is comfortable and inviting, with dark colors and chandeliers hanging above the casino floor. Since Bally is the leading maker of gaming machines, you'll find video versions of poker, blackjack, craps, and roulette (a great place to learn how to play). The showroom features the adults-only *Jubilee!*, while headliners have included everyone from Penn & Teller to Paul Anka. Try the Sterling Brunch. Behind the casino is a monorail running to the MGM Grand.

Bellagio

One of the most lavish resorts in Las Vegas is the **Bellagio Hotel and Casino**, a stunning replica of an Italian villa that boasted an equally stunning price tag: $1.6 billion dollars. Gaming rooms offer an unlikely quiet elegance, while the **Gallery of Fine Art** (open Sun–Thur 10am–6pm, Fri–

Glass ceiling

The iridescent glass sculpture over the lobby at Bellagio cost over $10m. It was made by Dale Chihuly, the first American accepted by the Italian glassmakers of Murano, near Venice.

Sat until 9pm) hosts traveling exhibitions. The dining is unparalleled, as are the luxurious accommodations. The conservatory features a lavish display of flowers, which changes with the seasons. One of the highlights of Vegas is the dazzling choreographed water show in the small lake fronting the resort, as well as Cirque du Soleil's remarkable aquatic show called O, although tickets don't come cheap and are booked out way in advance. Do note: shopping in the hall of retail fame that is Via Bellagio is for big spenders. Tiffany and Prada have stores here, and it is always fun to at least browse.

THE STRIP – NORTH

The northern Strip has changed even faster than its southern neighbor, and there is plenty to see and do. Tiny by Strip standards, but occupying a powerful corner of the famed boulevard is the 200-room **Bill's Gamblin' Hall and Saloon**. The rooms are very good value, offering a charming and comfortable rendition of 1900 San Francisco, but the real draw of the hotel-casino is the highly praised restaurant, Drai's on the Strip. Recognized as one of Las Vegas' best, Drai's arrived when Hollywood restaurateur Victor Drai took over the hotel's basement offering his own vision of the nouvelle French menu.

The venerable **Flamingo Las Vegas** retains Bugsy Siegel's original theme of a 'desert oasis' with a lushly restful tropical pool and garden area complete with swans, ducks, penguins and flamingos. Little of the older hotel remains, though Siegel is commemorated by a small plaque near the wedding garden. Amenities range from nine restaurants to five pools, six tennis courts, a health club and several boutiques. Most gaming tables offer low minimum bets, however, and slot junkies have a choice of more than 2,000 machines waiting to be fed.

Caesars Palace

A standard-setter since its 1968 opening, **Caesars Palace Hotel and Casino** is one of the few old-timers to keep pace with modern Las Vegas, perhaps because its ancient Rome

The Flamingo has a desert oasis theme

theme was popular from the outset (that, and the genuine marble never seems to go out of style). Here, elegance seems within anyone's reach, though having lots of money certainly helps. The casino is a high-roller's heaven with lofty limits at many tables. Sports fans will enjoy the lively environment at the Sports Book, where bets are placed on athletic events. Additional pleasantries include a fitness center and a spa. The popular and respected **Forum Shops** offers a fabulous spread of shopping, as well as dining for any budget, while the Omnimax Theatre and IMAX 3-D motion simulator ride, both located in the Forum Shops, are very popular with kids of any age.

The Paris Opera House at the Venetian

Imperial Palace and the Venetian

Recognizable by its blue-neon tinted pagoda, the sprawling **Imperial Palace Hotel and Casino** houses 2,700 rooms, 10 restaurants (including two buffets), and a 75,000-sq-ft (6,975-sq-m) casino. Aside from the gaming room, the most popular draws here are the *Legends In Concert* impersonation show and the **Imperial Palace Auto Collection** (open daily 9.30am–9.30pm), where collectable and historic automobiles are displayed. Check out Marilyn Monroe's convertible.

Harrah's Las Vegas is a profusion of bright colors, fiber-optic fireworks, tropical palm trees, and huge murals of international fêtes. It's a sizable establishment, with over 2,600 guest rooms and an enormous gaming area. Seven restaurants offer a welcome respite from the

Viva Venezia

Gondoliers were recruited from the ranks of boatmen in Venice, Italy, to ply the Venetian's Grand Canal at the casino's opening.

glitz, but the real fun is in The Improv comedy club, which showcases three new comedians each week.

The ornate, lovely **Venetian Resort Hotel-Casino** pushes the Italian-theming envelope. Renaissance Venice is evoked with dramatic replicas of the Doge's Palace, Campanile, and canals with gondolas and serenading gondoliers. It's an elegant, upscale resort with the renowned Canyon Ranch spa on its premises, and enough marble-and-stone flooring to cover a dozen football fields. The resort's capacity of 3,000 rooms has recently been expanded with the construction of another tower. A real centerpiece of the complex is the **Grand Canal Shoppes**, a collection of beautiful stores and restaurants.

The newly opened **Palazzo**, adjacent to the Venetian and under the same ownership, is one of several mixed-use developments that will transform the Strip over the next few years. Along with more than 3,000 luxury hotel suites, the Palazzo boasts the most expensive condominium units in the city. Hotel features include a polished marble lobby under a 60-foot dome with a two-story fountain, as well as seven interconnected swimming pools.

The Mirage

The pioneer of modern themed resorts, the **Mirage Hotel and Casino** shows some age when compared against the newer extravaganzas. Still, it is attractive to both high- and low-rollers, owing to a lush environment (think Maui on steroids) and stylish accommodations. The pool area is particularly pleasant.

Tigers gambol in the Secret Garden at the Mirage

Minimum bets start at $5 for blackjack and roulette, but there is plenty of free entertainment once you've blown your gambling budget. The Lagoon Saloon features live music in an indoor rain forest, while 11 restaurants feed the hungry masses with everything from buffet fare to gourmet cuisine. Left of the check-in desk is an incredible and mesmerizing aquarium.

Fronting the hotel is the famous Mirage volcano, belching flames and water to delight pedestrians. The big attraction here is the **Secret Garden and Dolphin Habitat**, roamed by Siegfried and Roy's famous white tigers. The duo of blond magicians put their wands away for the last time in 2003, when, on Roy Horn's birthday, October 3, the illusionist was savagely mauled during the show by one of the tigers. The tiger was making its debut appearance on that night. Roy's health is said to be progressing well, but no more public performances are planned. A larger-than-life statue of the duo stands in a plaza in front of the hotel.

T.I. (Treasure Island)

T.I. (Treasure Island) offers yet more affordable elegance. Though it looks very similar, Treasure Island is actually slightly lower-budget than its sister resort, the Mirage. As in the Mirage, betting limits start low and quickly rise as

the sun sets. Outside, a sea battle stops pedestrian traffic, raging nightly between a band of sexy sirens and a renegade group of pirates. The pirate theme was originally aimed at families, but bosses decided that grown-ups spent much more money, and in 2004 the resort underwent a rebranding exercise (from Treasure Island to 'T.I.'), to attract a more adult market.

The Desert Inn, a Las Vegas classic, was imploded in 2001 to make way for entrepreneur Steve Wynn's $1.6 billion fantasy, **Wynn Las Vegas**. Dominating this part of the Strip, the sweeping, shiny black resort is also home to the tycoon's fabulous art exhibition. The artworks are distributed throughout the hotel's common areas. The hotel also houses an indoor 'mountain', backed by a huge curtain waterfall that spills into a three-acre indoor lake. Behind the hotel lies an 18-hole championship golf course designed by Tom Fazio for the exclusive use of Wynn's guests. Buy golfing clothes at the Wynn Esplanade and you can guarantee they'll be designed by Dior, Chanel or John-Paul Gaultier.

Circus Circus

First of the family-friendly low-roller casinos over two decades ago, **Circus Circus Hotel and Casino** shows signs of fatigue. However, families still appreciate the free circus acts every half-hour from 11am to midnight, the carnival games, arcade, and giant indoor amusement park, **Adventuredome**.

Circus Circus – family fun

The huge casino area is separated into three areas, connected by walkways and a monorail. To watch the circus acts, just look up from your slot machine. Compared to the rest of the Strip, Circus Circus is a throwback that attracts low-rollers looking for cheap thrills. The present owner, MGM Mirage, has announced that it will close the Circus Circus RV park, demolish the older part of the hotel, and rebuild a much larger Circus Circus on the site.

Riviera Hotel

When it opened in 1955, the nine-story **Riviera Hotel and Casino** was the Strip's first high-rise, styled after the luxury resorts of the Côte d'Azur. The days of Liberace and Orson Welles gracing the showroom are long gone, and today's Riviera attracts a less stellar clientele. Piecemeal expansion has left a confusing layout. There are 2,100 guest rooms, and restaurants include the upscale Kristofer's Steakhouse. There are swimming pools, tennis courts, and a small shopping area, but the real attractions are the adult live shows. Some showgirls are immortalized by a bronze sculpture of their rear-ends.

The Sahara and the Stratosphere

Built in 1952, the **Sahara Hotel and Casino** underwent a $100-million renovation, transforming it to a themed Moroccan palace. The renovation replaced the dark and plush atmosphere with a lighter decor, and the result has been one of comfort, suitable for tour groups, conventioneers, and mid-budget travelers. Close to 2,000 rooms and 75,000 sq ft (6,975 sq m) of gaming surround a beautiful pool area. The Sahara's NASCAR **Cyber Speedway** offers Indy-car racing simulation, but skip the buffet, which does not get high marks. Though the casino area is not elegant, the minimum limits are low, and the pit bosses can be more relaxed and good-humored than elsewhere on the Strip.

The **Stratosphere Hotel and Casino** and its soaring **Stratosphere Tower** struggle against the challenges of location – too far north for the Strip, too far south for Downtown, The complex sports a faint World's Fair theme, but it's definitely a vast improvement over Vegas World, the universally loathed hotel it replaced.

The hotel's centerpiece is the 1,149-ft (350-m) tower, which includes a 109th-floor observation deck (one of the highest in the US), an 83rd-floor revolving restaurant with reasonable food, and four thrill rides (the **Big Shot** and **X-Scream** are truly frightening experiences).

Along with the requisite gaming area – which is well thought of for its loose slots and low-limit tables – are seven restaurants, over 40 stores, and the *American Superstars* impersonator show. Lovers with stars in their eyes can get hitched in the **Chapel in the Clouds**, which hovers 100 stories above the Strip.

The Stratosphere Tower

The Fremont Street Experience uses 2 million light bulbs

DOWNTOWN

While the wonders of the Strip eclipsed Downtown early in the city's history, the area still has much to offer visitors. Both the city's oldest casino (El Cortez) and its oldest hotel (the Golden Gate, where Las Vegas's first telephone was installed) are located Downtown, as are numerous other properties, including magnate Steve Wynn's first, the Golden Nugget.

Until recently, Fremont Street was Las Vegas's civic gathering spot, home to holiday parades and the Wild-West-themed Helldorado festival. Over time, the shopping moved to the suburbs and the attorneys moved to high-rise offices just outside the gaming area. In the face of stagnating revenues, local Downtown government and business owners have tried to explore ways to increase traffic to the famed district. One lure has been the opening of **Las Vegas Premium Outlets**, just off Interstate 15 and Charleston Boulevard.

Fremont Street Experience

The incredible **Fremont Street Experience** is one of the area's greatest draws. The combined project of casino owners and the city, this part of Fremont Street, between Las Vegas Boulevard and Main Street, was closed to traffic and landscaped into a pedestrian mall at an original cost of $70 million. The Experience's most impressive feature is the 90-ft (2.75-m) high vaulted canopy that plays host to **Viva Vision**, a three-block-long audio-visual show, said to be the world's largest (shows every hour, starting at dusk). Between the hourly 15-minute light shows, live musicians offer free entertainment on two stages. Apart from making the area friendlier, the Experience also cleaned up the Downtown city blocks – at least the part under its influence.

The Experience was later joined by a non-gaming entertainment complex called **Neonopolis**. The $99-million complex features the multi-screen Crown Movie Theaters, restaurants, shopping and underground parking, with lots more to come, they hope. It is part of the **Fremont East Entertainment District**, recently refurbished with an array of vintage neon signs. More than a dozen new clubs and restaurants opened here in 2007.

Fremont is a throwback to the old days of Las Vegas gaming. House gambling rules are generally more flexible, allowing for both lower minimum bets and higher limits (sometimes even no-limit gaming). Additionally, there is a certain rough quality to Downtown, an experience different than that offered at the shiny new Strip resorts. Do not mistake this edginess for danger; the Fremont Street Experience has done quite a bit to im-

Light fantastic

12.5 million LEDs and a 550,000-watt sound system deliver the dazzling spectacle of Viva Vision. The moving picture show features jet fighters, exotic birds, and dancing girls.

Into the future

The monorail that links casinos on the Strip is planned to eventually reach all the way to Downtown's city blocks.

prove the safety of the area, sometimes drawing the ire of civil rights and free speech activists. Darker reaches off the beaten track of central Downtown are still considered unwise for tourists, though.

Main Street Station and the Plaza

Main Street Station is perhaps Downtown's best-kept secret. Just north of the Fremont Street Experience, this Victorian-styled casino fulfills the promise of the exterior architecture and gas-fired street lamps with a detailed interior filled with antiques. Unlike other casinos, Main Street showcases genuine articles; a carved Scottish fireplace and Teddy Roosevelt's Pullman car among them. Dining includes the upscale Pullman Grille for steak and seafood, and the Triple 7 Brewpub for handcrafted ales and wood-fired pizza.

The neon **Plaza Hotel and Casino** is located at the west end of the Fremont Street Experience canopy. It has a dark, smoky, 1970s feel, and has always been a maverick of hotel-casinos, featuring in many of the '70s-era Vegas movies. With just over 1,000 rooms and a 75,000-sq-ft (6,975-sq-m) gaming area that includes penny slots, the Plaza attracts an interesting mix of friendly gamblers and seniors. The showroom offers campy, adult-oriented revues.

Hotel California and Lady Luck

The name of the **California Hotel and Casino** is misleading. The people who run this off-Fremont Street hotel-casino on Ogden Avenue spend most of their marketing budget in Hawaii, attracting islanders by the planeload who provide up to 85 percent of the casino's business. Consequently, the theme is the South Seas, and the four restaurants feature

Will lady luck shine on you?

Hawaiian dishes and drinks. There is a Hawaiian specialty gift store for souvenirs, and 781 modestly priced rooms aimed squarely at the budget traveler.

The **Lady Luck Casino Hotel** on North Third Street went a long way toward preserving the glitzy Las Vegas of old, with its handsome collection of neon, mirrors, and brass. Unfortunately, this was not enough to lure gamblers away from the thundering attractions Uptown, and in early 2006 it closed for extensive renovations. Noone knows if it will reopen.

Fremont Street Casinos

The **Las Vegas Club Hotel and Casino**, one of the oldest casinos in Las Vegas, marks the beginning of the Fremont Experience canopy. Explore 40,000 sq ft (3,720 sq m) of gaming with some of the most liberal house rules in town. The modest theming here features a widely dispersed exhibition of sports memorabilia, as well as card dealers dressed in jersey-like uniforms. The hotel tower was added in 1980 and features 410 affordable, comfortable rooms. There are also three casual restaurants.

The San Francisco-styled **Golden Gate Hotel and Casino** has stood at One Fremont Street since 1906. The charming operation is the city's oldest hotel, the home of its first telephone, and the original purveyor of the classic shrimp cocktail. Its 106 small but pleasant rooms with plaster walls and mahogany doors hark back to another era, and its coffee shop is an original, if not too classy, Downtown experience. Piano players entertain with infectious ragtime.

The only prominent Downtown hotel-casino without a multicolored neon sign (though its facade is completely covered with small golden lightbulbs), the 1946 **Golden Nugget**, was remodeled as Steve Wynn's first hotel project in 1987. Metropolitan elegance supersedes the surrounding glitz.

The Golden Nugget's shimmering facade

Guests, greeted by uniformed doormen, enter a gilded lobby full of marble and crystal. The guest rooms and misted pool area landscaped with palms are fancy

enough to have earned good ratings. The Golden Nugget showroom offers headliners and production shows; there are four restaurants as well, including a top-notch mid-priced buffet and two more formal dining rooms.

4 Queens

A blinding neon landmark since 1966, the **4 Queens Hotel and Casino** today mainly attracts older guests, many of whom are repeat customers. A 12-seat blackjack table (the world's largest) and a giant slot machine draw players to the 60,000-sq ft (5,580-sq-m) casino. The 700 rooms of earthtone decor are pleasant and affordable. Its four restaurants include Hugo's Cellar, an always-busy classic Las Vegas gourmet room with a winning wine list.

Fitzgerald's Casino and Hotel is the Las Vegas lowrollers' gaming haven. Once the tallest building in Nevada at 34 stories, Fitzgerald's 650 rooms offer terrific views of the city and the mountains. Accommodations are of the national chain-hotel variety, and priced accordingly, ie, not expensive, as are the numerous restaurants and bars.

Binion's Gambling Hall and Hotel

Founded by gambler Benny Binion, **Binion's Gambling Hall and Hotel** may be the most traditional, old-school gaming joint left in town. The casino has some of the highest betting limits in Vegas, and no-limit gaming. Billed as 'the Place that Made Poker Famous,' the family-run Binion's hosted the World Series of Poker for many action-packed years, until

Binion's, a bastion of tradition

Becky Binion sold the casino in 2004. The Binion family come from Texas ranching stock, so premium beef is on offer in the coffeeshop and the Ranch Steak House.

The **Fremont Hotel and Casino** was one of Las Vegas' first high-rises, built in 1956, and is famous for launching Wayne Newton's career. The hotel no longer has a showroom, but 452 modest guest rooms accommodate the Hawaiian travelers who frequent the place. The Fremont's block-long signage helps turn Downtown night into day, and the Second Street Grill is a hidden gem, featuring Pacific Rim specialties.

As Las Vegas experienced record growth and continued a trend toward the implosion of its older resorts, a desire arose to preserve some of the city's history. Neon signage is perhaps the single most recognizable icon of Las Vegas. So, the **Neon Museum** has assumed the responsibility of raising funds to restore some of the rusting signs from the past and display them in their glory. Neon signs have been installed on posts in the Fremont Street area and around Neonopolis, as the Neon Museum itself has no permanent premises.

El Cortez

Unrivaled for its continuous parade of low-stakes gamblers, **El Cortez Hotel and Casino** (built in 1941) is the city's oldest continuously operating casino. A $20-million top-to-bottom renovation has created new luxury suites alongside the original modest rooms. The relatively large casino still features single-deck blackjack, 'loose' slots, and absurdly low limits, though many of the penny and nickel machines of yesteryear have been removed to make the floor less congested. Dining options include a conventional steakhouse and one of the city's most affordable breakfast buffets. There are 402 rooms at remarkably low prices.

Art District

South of Fremont Street, centered around the intersection of Main and Charleston, the **18b Art District** has the city's largest concentration of artists' studios and galleries. The district comes alive each month for First Friday evening celebrations, as well as all-day Art About festivals on the third Saturday of the month.

Local art on display

In the heart of the district is the **Arts Factory** complex (open Mon–Tues and Thur–Fri noon–5pm; tel: 702-676 1111), located on East Charleston Boulevard. An old warehouse converted into artists' studios, this place is a touch of SoHo in Sin City and the lynchpin of a growing Downtown arts scene. Inside are various galleries that exhibit avant garde art including the Contemporary Arts Collective (tel: 702-382 3886; call before you visit to check current opening hours).

The Rio Casino at twilight

WEST OF THE STRIP

Las Vegas has been described as 'Des Moines with casinos,' and to a certain extent that is true – beyond the glitter of the Strip, the quality of attractions pales somewhat. But there are still intriguing stops worth a visitor's time and effort. And while most hotel-casinos and resorts are concentrated along the Strip and within the Downtown area, some are found just off the Strip. To the west are recently developed resort corridors off both Flamingo Road and Tropicana Avenue.

These areas consist primarily of light industrial development with sparse housing or apartments nearby. To the east of the Strip is the convention area of Paradise Road, offering – in addition to traditional hotel-casinos – a spate of non-gaming business-oriented hotels as well as a developing restaurant row. Here are some of the highlights of the properties and attractions to the West of the Strip.

West Flamingo Road

Three different kinds of casinos are located on West Flamingo Road. The **Rio All-Suite Resort and Casino** offers a variety of quality mid-priced amenities. There are 2,556 rooms in total, and the standard accommodations are among the city's largest. The **Masquerade Village** is a Carnivale-themed collection of gaming, retail outlets and restaurants, while the **Voodoo Lounge** is a top-floor cocktail lounge with citywide views. The casino floor, lorded over by serious-looking pit bosses wearing laughably gaudy tropical wear, is packed with locals and tourists, especially on weekends. Five-dollar minimum bets are standard. After the night's last performance, the showroom turns into the Club Rio disco, a popular late-night dancing spot.

The Palms

Worth a trip away from the Strip, **The Palms** has an understated Polynesian theme and is decorated in soft beiges and taupes. Check out the **ghostbar** for stylish elegance, as well as the sensuous hotel pool and the tropical spa treatments. The hotel attracts a good-looking, well-heeled clientele. The Palms also boasts a full recording studio, a high-tech concert hall and the world's last operating Playboy Club.

The Palms

Gold Coast

Offering a combination of entertainment and gaming, the **Gold Coast Hotel and Casino** fulfills many traditional Las Vegas expectations. On site is a 70-lane bowling center, a lounge with karaoke, and a dance hall that regularly features live big-band, swing, and rockabilly music. Dining rooms are varied and inexpensive, and the swimming pool is popular. But the true resort draw is in the huge number of video poker machines, which attract mainly locals, despite the 740 hotel rooms.

Orleans

The showy facade of the **Orleans Hotel and Casino** on West Tropicana Avenue, is a little misleading and overbearing; once you enter, the decor is rather subtle. The casino is more akin to a warehouse than the Big Easy, but the 50-ft (15-m) ceilings do well to eradicate the typical smoky, claustrophobic atmosphere. A 70-lane bowling center and multi-screen movie theater attract locals, while the 14 casual restaurants, the 9,000-seat arena and the 827-seat showroom (featuring well-known performers from the past, like Bobby Rydell and Debbie Reynolds) should appeal to anyone seeking fun on a budget.

Conventions

With a recent major expansion, the Las Vegas Convention Center became one of the largest convention centers in the world. COMDEX and the Consumer Electronics Show – in the fall and winter – are particularly popular events. Other major conventions include gatherings of the adult-entertainment industry, automobile accessory marketers, fashion companies, and even pizza-equipment industries.

The obvious financial benefit of the influx of conventioneers is offset by snarled traffic, inflated room rates, and packed attractions. Some merchants – and most taxi drivers – complain that conventioneers are less free-spending than vacationers. Nevertheless, city planners continue to woo the convention trade, with several Strip resorts building their own centers, and new ones springing up in the valley.

Inside the Las Vegas Convention Center

EAST OF THE STRIP

For all its reputation as a vacation hot-spot, Las Vegas also enjoys success as a major convention destination. Every week companies, industries, and lifestyle organizations arrive en masse from all over the world to mix business with pleasure. How vital are such trade shows to the city economy? Enough so that many Las Vegas resorts – such as Mandalay Bay – have elaborate convention facilities, as do suburbs like Henderson.

The king, however, remains the **Las Vegas Convention Center**. A recent expansion added 51 meeting rooms, a 500-seat restaurant and state-of-the-art technology. It is also within walking distance of more than 50,000 hotel rooms, one of the center's main attractions.

The **Las Vegas Hilton Hotel and Casino** – next to the Convention Center – is perfect for lovers of large-scale resorts catering to every need. Public areas are graciously decorated and there are 3,174 plush guest rooms. Amenities include a spa, six lighted tennis courts, 12 restaurants, and a showroom and lounge featuring top talent. Hilton highlights are a huge sports betting floor *Star Trek: The Experience*, a permanent high-tech attraction featuring futuristic gaming, dining, and its centerpiece interactive amusement ride. Proximity to the convention building means the Hilton's occupancy and rates rise during conventions, so book in advance. The Hilton stands on the site of the old International Hotel, where Elvis Presley performed before sold-out audiences for years, and a statue of The King stands in the lobby.

Liberace Museum

Liberace may no longer be with us, but Mr Showmanship's absolutely fabulous cars, gilded pianos, and indescribable

The Liberace Museum is a study in excess

costumes can still be seen at the **Liberace Museum** on East Tropicana Avenue (tel: 702-384 3466, open Mon–Sat 10am–5pm; Sun 1–5pm). The jewel of the entertainer's collection may in fact be a fake jewel – a 50-pound rhinestone, said to be the world's largest. This shrine to one of America's most popular and campiest pianists won't disappoint.

The Hard Rock

The Hard Rock

One of the more notable hotels in Las Vegas not located on the Strip is the **Hard Rock Hotel and Casino** on Paradise Road. A surprising exercise in casual elegance, considering its theme, this experiment a few years ago, aimed at the younger market, has resulted in a rebirth of the glory days of Vegas. If you're wondering where many of the hip and pretty people hang out, this is it. Guitars of the stars and other music memorabilia are on display everywhere: there are vintage gold records on the walls, and even the light fixtures are cymbals. Hardwood flooring surrounds the handsome casino – slot machine handles, for example, are shaped like Fender Stratocaster guitar necks – while performers of every musical style attract full houses in the 1,200-seat club-style showroom. Dining includes the casual, cantina-style Pink Taco, and a branch of the achingly stylish Japanese eatery, Nobu. A lush pool area greets sunbathers, and rooms are spacious and tasteful, with celebrity photos on the walls, big flat-screen TVs, and Bose sound systems. Expansion doubled the property's amenities, but has not destroyed the hotel's reputation.

Mammoth kidding around at the Nevada State Museum

CULTURAL ATTRACTIONS

Las Vegas is gunning hard to establish itself as a center for the arts, but even though the city's history is short, its past is not being neglected. There are several institutes devoted to Las Vegas history, including the **Nevada State Museum and Historical Society** on Twin Lakes Drive (tel: 702-486 5205), and the **Clark County Heritage Museum** on South Boulder Highway (tel: 702-455 7955). The Nevada State Museum has an excellent woolly mammoth display, of the variety that used to live in Nevada.

The **Las Vegas Natural History Museum** (900 Las Vegas Boulevard North, tel: 702-384 3466) is large on reptiles and snakes. Visitors to the **Old Mormon Fort Historic Park** (southeast corner of Las Vegas Boulevard and Washington, tel: 702-486 3511) can see remnants of the city's oldest building, a fort built by original Mormon settlers in 1855. All four museums are open daily 9am–4pm. There's plenty to engage adults, too, at the **Lied Discovery Children's Museum** (833 Las Vegas Boulevard North, tel: 702-382 3445, open Mon–Sat 10am–5pm, Sun 1–5pm).

Ranking high among the city's family-oriented attractions, the newly opened **Las Vegas Springs Preserve** (333 South Valley View Road, tel: 702-822 7700, open Mon–Thur 10am–6pm, Fri–Sun 10am–10pm) features a recreation of the original springs that made the Las Vegas Valley an oasis before it was a town, complete with 'flash floods' of re-circulated water. Five buildings are filled with interactive exhibits on the challenges of using water wisely in the desert. There is a small arboretum of cactuses from various North American deserts, as well as 180 acres of natural desert with hiking trails.

Art Museums

At the Venetian is one of the classiest museums in the West, the **Guggenheim Hermitage Museum** (tel: 702-360 8000, open daily 9am–11pm). The Guggenheim Hermitage, in conjunction with the prestigious New York and Russian museums of the same name, showcases works by great masters such as Camille Pisarro, Vincent Van Gogh, Paul Gauguin, Henri Rousseau, Paul Cezanne, Pierre Auguste Renoir, Peter Paul Rubens, and Rembrandt, as well as modern art superstars like Robert Mapplethorpe, in rotating exhibits from both museums' collections.

Across town on West Sahara Avenue is the **Las Vegas Art Museum** (tel: 702-360 8000, open Tues–Sat 10am–5pm, Sun 1–5pm). The museum, attached to the Sahara West Library, is large and designed to the exacting specifications of the Smithsonian Institute. Curators schedule a mix of local and touring shows, often including work by recognized masters.

The University of Nevada, Las Vegas

The **University of Nevada at Las Vegas** (UNLV) and the **Community College of Southern Nevada** have been unofficial outposts of beyond-the-neon culture since their inception. UNLV's sprawling urban campus on South Maryland Parkway has quite a collection of interesting sights and venues.

The **Marjorie Barrick Museum** (tel: 702-895 3381, open Mon–Fri 8am–4.45pm, Sat 10am–2pm) is a natural history museum with live lizards, gila monsters, tortoises, and a red snake, as well as stuffed birds. There are also some good exhibits on the arts and crafts of the Paiute, Navajo, and Mexican Native Americans.

Just outside the entrance is the campus **Xeric Garden**, a landscaped sampling of desert plants in a beautiful setting. The **Donna Beam Fine Arts Gallery** (tel: 702-895 3893, open Mon–Fri 9am–5pm, Sat 10am–2pm) is a spacious hall exhibiting the work of students as well as professionals. Also on campus is the **Artemus Ham Concert Hall** (tel: 702-895 3801), featuring classical, rock, and theatrical performances, and the **Thomas and Mack Center**, an arena with 18,000 seats, that hosts everything from hockey to rodeos and musical events. On the Community College campus at 3200 East Cheyenne Avenue is the city's only **planetarium** (tel: 702-651 4759), where the latest digital technology is used to project views of planets and stars, as well as 3D films, onto their domed screen.

A Maya vase at the Marjorie Barrick Museum

Lake Mead is perfect for outdoor recreation most of the year

EXCURSIONS

Hoover Dam and Lake Mead

There is much to do within easy driving distance of Las Vegas, from recreation to sightseeing. Easily the top draw is the **Hoover Dam**, responsible for Las Vegas's first major crowd (of 20,000), who attended its 1935 dedication. Long after its completion, the dam remains an awe-inspiring sight, living up to its old billing as the 'Eighth Wonder of the World.'

Striking sculptures by Oskar J.W. Hansen may be the largest monumental bronzes ever cast in the US. A dizzying 725ft (526m) high, this engineering marvel straddles the Nevada-Arizona border a half-hour's drive south of Las Vegas on US93. The **Hoover Dam Visitors Center** is open daily from 9am to 6pm, tel: 702-294 3524, but the last tour is around 4pm. Since the September 11, 2001 tragedy, the tours inside the dam have been suspended, but a two-hour discovery tour has been in-

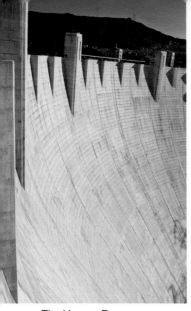
The Hoover Dam

troduced for the one million visitors who come here each year. Visitors are also prohibited from carrying purses, daypacks or anything else larger than a camera onto the dam. No pets allowed either.

The man-made result of Hoover Dam, **Lake Mead** offers more than 500 miles (800km) of shoreline in the midst of a 1.5-million-acre (607,000-hectare) national recreation area. A popular spot for locals and visitors alike, America's largest man-made body of water is open all year (peak usage month is June). Activities include fishing, swimming, water-skiing, boating, self-guided hiking, camping, and picnicking. Boats can be rented at the **Lake Mead Marina** or the **Echo Bay Marina**. Lake Mead Cruises (tel: 702-293 6180; ask about hotel pick-up) offers a variety of excursions, including a sunset dinner cruise with surprisingly good food. The company can schedule trips around the lake on Jet Skis, as well as on a fast-paced jet-boat that heads in the direction of the Grand Canyon. The lake is best reached through Henderson, 10–15 minutes from the Strip by freeway, or Boulder City, a half-hour drive south of Las Vegas.

Boulder City

Boulder City itself is an anomaly in Nevada – a city that rejects gaming and discourages excessive growth. Its small-town feel is quaint and charming by the standards of booming suburban southern Nevada.

The heart of the town is a historic square, fronted by 1930s-era buildings such as the **Boulder Dam Hotel** and the **Boulder Dam Theatre**. The hotel houses several galleries, stores, and an attractive restaurant, while the town is home to several art galleries and antiques shops; call the Chamber of Commerce, tel: 702-293 2034 for details. Also worth seeing is the **Hoover Dam Museum** (tel: 702-294 1988, open daily 10am–5pm, Sun noon–5pm), which is well-stocked with artifacts from the building of the dam and the founding of Boulder City. In the fall, several festivals, including Art in the Park and Damboree (a celebration of the town's heritage), entice thousands to abandon the gaming tables and make the trek from Las Vegas. Take US93 south about 25 miles (40km) from Vegas; Hoover Dam is an additional 7 miles (11km).

Ghost Towns

While not really a ghost town, **Goodsprings** has the feel of a genuinely spooky place. The functioning homes are surrounded by mill foundations and abandoned mine operations. The hamlet's chief attraction is the Pioneer Saloon, the country's largest stamped-metal building. Head south from Las Vegas on Interstate 15 and turn at the tiny town of **Jean**.

The true and authentic ghost town of **Rhyolite** is located 126 miles (200km) northwest of Las Vegas on US95. Once Nevada's second-largest city, thanks to a 1904 gold strike, remnants can be seen in the Tonopah–Las Vegas Railroad depot. A

Living ghost town

Calico Ghost Town (open daily 8am–dusk), near Barstow in California, has been restored as a themed amusement park where visitors can take train rides and see silver-mine tunnels.

top attraction is the 'bottle house,' built of 50,000 glass bottles, common practice in the days of scarce building supplies. Just outside town is an unlikely cluster of large Belgian sculptures including Albert Szukalski's *Last Supper* (a re-creation of the da Vinci masterpiece using plaster ghosts as the Disciples), a 28-ft (8.5-m) miner, and a 25-ft (7.5-m) female nude built of cinder blocks.

Valley of Fire State Park

Fifty miles (80km) northeast of Las Vegas via Interstate 15 (watch for the Valley of Fire exit, State Route 169), **Valley of Fire State Park** is a spectacular alien landscape of erosion-sculpted, brilliant red sandstone. The park features Native petroglyphs dating to 300BC, most accessible by light hikes. Atlatl Rock has a stairway to the carvings, while the glyphs at Mouse's Tank require an easy quarter-mile (0.5-km) trek. For the car-bound, there is a 6-mile (9.5-km) scenic loop through White Domes, a stunning vista of sandstone formations that were once the bottom of an inland sea. There are also some picnic areas and overnight campgrounds. The park is best visited in late spring or fall.

Spectacularly eroded rocks in the Valley of Fire State Park

In nearby Overton, the **Lost City Museum** (721 South Moapa Road, tel: 702-397 2193, open daily 8.30am–4.30pm) preserves the ruins of Pueblo Grande de Nevada, the state's largest ancient Anasazi community, which was moved here brick by adobe brick before its original site was flooded by Lake Mead.

The desolate beauty of Red Rock Canyon

Red Rock Canyon

Red Rock Canyon National Conservation Area, a half-hour drive west of downtown Las Vegas via Charleston Boulevard, is a dramatic vista of mountains and colorful sheer rock faces. Rather than just a single canyon, it is a 13-mile (21-km) ridge with canyons eroded into its flanks. First stop should be the **Red Rock Visitors Center** (tel: 702-363 1921, open daily until 4.30pm), which has archaeological displays and dioramas depicting the lives of early native inhabitants. At Willow Spring, well-preserved petroglyphs can still be seen.

Starting at the center, the one-way scenic loop meanders through the area's stunning topography, but when driving on the loop, watch out for bicyclists. Picnicking spaces are plentiful, as are hiking trails of varying levels of difficulty. During migratory seasons, bird watchers can have a field day. The canyon is one of the nation's top rock-climbing sites, with an almost endless variety of ascents, but novices should stick to an appropriate level; rescuers are frequently called out to help find lost or injured visitors.

Mount Charleston

For a cool break from the desert, try 11,918-ft (3,632-m) **Charleston Peak**, near the town of **Mount Charleston**, 40 minutes north of Las Vegas on US95. Two areas command particular attention: Kyle Canyon and Lee Canyon. Kyle is home to scenic Cathedral Rock, Mary Jane Falls, and Big Falls, all accessible by trail (Cathedral Rock requires a three-hour trek). Lee Canyon is home to a ski and snowboarding resort, remarkable for being so near the desert. The mountain features numerous scenic overlooks and picnicking sites, while the ranger station on Kyle Canyon Road can provide advice.

Grand Canyon

There are several noteworthy national parks within driving distance of Las Vegas. The most famous and most popular is the **Grand Canyon**. The North Rim is 280 miles (448km) east of

Grand Canyon

One of the world's most spectacular natural phenomena, the Grand Canyon averages 10 miles (16km) wide and reaches depths of 5,700ft (1,700m). It transects five of the seven temperate zones, each with its own unique ecology. Declared a National Park in 1919, the canyon was 'discovered' by Lieutenant Joseph Ives in 1857, who called it a 'pointless locality.'

The canyon has been created over millions of years by the erosion of the great Colorado River. From the lookout points at the rim of the canyon, the river seems little more than a trickling stream. Climbing within designated areas is encouraged: strata of red-and-yellow sandstone sandwich layers of dark granite and pale limestone, revealing the surrounding earth's structure and layers of evolution.

Las Vegas; the South Rim 260 miles (416km) from Vegas. There are no connecting bridges across the divide. The **South Rim**, accessible by Interstate 40 through the state of Arizona, is the most visited area of the park. It is also closest to the **Skywalk**, an awe-inspiring glass-floored platform suspended 4,000 feet above the Colorado River. The **North Rim** – arrived at by Interstate 15 through St George, Utah – receives a fraction of that traffic because of the longer journey times. The stunning natural wonder makes an ideal excursion far away from Sin City's glitz. Driving there

The Grand Canyon

is the preferable option, for having a car gives access to outstanding scenic overlooks; also access to good walking trails, although, as one visitors' guide says, they are 'narrow and close to the edge,' so agility is desirable. For anyone in a hurry, though, it's possible to take an organized airplane or helicopter charter trip and return to Vegas the same day.

Rafting and Mule Tours

For active travelers, the park offers backpacking, rafting, and mule-back descents into the canyon. Back-country hiking requires an advance permit; hikes down to the river generally take two days or more, and returning even longer. For more sedentary visitors, there are historic sites to visit, star-gazing,

Rafting the Colorado River

bird-watching, and, of course, enough spectacular scenery to keep all eyes constantly busy. To travel down into the canyon, plan ahead, and make all your arrangements well in advance.

As for weather, both rims receive snow in the winter, and even summer evenings may be chilly. Due to climate conditions, the North Rim is open only May to October. Down in the canyon, more desert-like conditions prevail, with summer afternoons approaching 120°F (49°C). For more information, tel: 520-638 7864, or call the Las Vegas Convention and Visitors Authority, tel: 702-892 0711.

Zion and Bryce Canyon National Parks

Northeast, in Utah, are the spectacular Zion and Bryce Canyon national parks. Around 155 miles (248km) from Las Vegas, en route to the North Rim of the Grand Canyon, **Zion Canyon** offers natural wonders such as stark rock formations, sheer cliff faces, and rippling waterfalls. The park, accessible year-round, offers hiking trails and scenic drives.

Farther north – 210 miles (336km) from Las Vegas – is **Bryce Canyon**, an amazing series of natural amphitheaters scooped from the edge of the Paunsagunt Plateau by the Paria River. Bryce is known for its colorful formations of sculptured rock – pinnacles, pedestals, fins, and spires. Sinking Ship, Thor's Hammer, and Natural Bridge, an awesome arch of rock, are just a sample of the canyon's spectacular geological sights.

Great Basin National Park

A five-hour drive from Vegas ends in **Great Basin National Park**, located along the Nevada-Utah state line. It is well worth the trip to the 77,000 acres (31,160 hectares) of rugged back country, with its groves of ancient bristlecone pine trees and the Lehman Caves, the premier limestone cavern system in the western USA. Head north by using interstates 93 and 50, and state highways 487 and 488.

Death Valley

Death Valley, presumed to be the last resting place of many a gold and silver prospector – actually, only one is known to have died – is 145 miles (232km) west of Las Vegas. Take US95 northwest or Interstate 15 south to Baker, California to get there. Death Valley's many popular destinations include Furnace Creek (which, with a gas station, hotels, and a golf course, is the only dot of civilization), the Devil's Golf Course, Zabriskie Point – immortalized in an arthouse movie of the same name – and the improbable Spanish-Mediterranean Scotty's Castle, completed in 1931 and which, at one time required the labor of 2,000 workmen. The Death Valley National Park Visitors Center can provide maps and information.

Sand dunes in Death Valley

WHAT TO DO

Whatever your taste in entertainment and recreation, Las Vegas has something to divert and delight you. From circuses to cocktail bars, from roller coasters to rock and roll, comedy to clubbing, the list is truly endless and the standards are stellar. Gambling may be the main event here, but the sideshows are spectacular.

Cirque du Soleil set a trend by having an auditorium built around its fabulous show, and Las Vegas resident Celine Dion followed their lead; the Colosseum theater opened at Caesars Palace designed exclusively around her act. Ms Dion later shared the bill with Elton John, and Bette Midler began her residency at the Colosseum in February 2008.

Until recently, the entertainment in Las Vegas was seen by the casinos as just an adjunct to the gaming. In fact, when Elvis started his 1969 residency at The International (now the Las Vegas Hilton), it was reportedly the first time that a casino made a profit in the showroom.

Now, Las Vegas reaps the rewards and suffers the losses of a metropolis of over one million residents whose primary industry is tourism. This makes the traditional travelers' definitions of 'what to do' and 'where to go' difficult to delineate. In this town, the two overlap. Casinos, resorts, gambling, and entertainment: where does one stop and the next begin? In Sin City they are interrelated, interconnected, and interdependent.

With the overwhelming population explosion that started in the late 1980s came a demand from the locals for more traditional,

Fremont Street by night

Vegas street life

People-watching is great free entertainment in Las Vegas. Many locals favor the benches by GameWorks to do it.

off-Strip experiences, sparking a growth in culture, sports, and amenities. That process is still young but steadily evolving. Locals and visitors are each feeling their way along a new path for experiencing Las Vegas, one that combines the expected attractions of the gaming and tourism industry with those types of independent cultural and sports amenities found in a more traditional city. The pleasurable result is a combination of the expected and the unexpected.

GAMBLING

Since 1931, when gambling was officially legalized in Nevada after 22 years of prohibition, it has been used to promote the city. Without question, the primary allure of Las Vegas – despite the resorts, restaurants, showrooms, and shopping malls – is the fact that you can legally place bets on games of chance and sporting events. Make no mistake: the times may be changing, but without gambling, there would be no Forum Shops, no pirate ships, no Guggenheim museums of art.

Most of the gambling in Las Vegas is concentrated along the Strip, where nearly 20 major casinos in excess of 100,000 sq ft (9,300 sq m) beckon passers-by to lighten their pockets a little or a lot and take the chance that they may be among the few who will win the 'Big One.'

At most gaming tables along the Strip, action is fast and furious, with generally inflexible house rules. Downtown casinos are a bit more flexible when it comes to house rules, offering lower minimums and higher (sometimes no) limits. This attracts the unlikely combination of serious career gamblers and novices without much to spend. Still, the atmosphere is generally

Collect your chips

Many casinos issue special chips for events like New Year, and players often prefer to collect them than cash them in.

Hoping to win big at the Imperial Palace Casino

more relaxed and amiable, probably due to the fact that Downtown is a concentrated area similar to a small town – one that has not changed much in 70 years. Still, before you venture into any live gaming area, it is important to familiarize yourself with the rules of the game.

Despite the exceptions mentioned above, most experienced gamblers have little patience for the novice, as they see them as a bad omen in the already frustrating situation of having to beat odds that are set against them. Also, there are strict rules regarding what the player should do with their cards and chips, and where they can place their hands. Disobeying these rules can cost you a bet on the low end; repeated violations can lead to expulsion from the casino.

Card Schools

If you are completely inexperienced, there are several ways to overcome your lack of knowledge. The first is to read

Blackjack is the easiest card game to learn

about the games. Below is a very brief guide to the most popular games, while books are available to explain the more complex rules. Another method is to practice on the video versions of these games before moving to live table action. With minimum wagers as low as 5¢ and no other players waiting impatiently for you to make your next move, electronic gaming is an alternative that many novice gamblers never move beyond. Most casinos offer a variety of video game slot machines.

Despite the potentially intimidating aspects of live gaming, it makes little sense to spend your vacation in Las Vegas and not play at least a few hands of blackjack or craps, especially when there are free gaming lessons offered at several different casinos. Dealers teach groups who have more-or-less equal ability, so no one feels pressured or out of place. This hands-on method is the best way to learn a game and its rules without risking your money or your pride.

Baccarat

Typically assumed to be a high-roller card game, baccarat *(bah-cah-rah)* is similar to blackjack, though it's played with stricter rules, higher limits, and less player interaction. The object of the game is to come as close as possible to 9; the only real skill involved is deciding whether to bet on the player or the bank (ie the dealer). Most baccarat tables are located in quiet, sequestered sections of the casino. Gambling lessons are highly recommended for this game.

Big 6 (or Money Wheel)

This spin-and-win game resembles a prize game offered in the carnivals of old. The game is easy – simply bet on one of the numbers – which makes it attractive to novices, but the house edge makes them leave equally quickly, and usually poorer.

Bingo

Nearly everyone knows the game of bingo, the mini-lottery in which players try to line up a horizontal or a vertical row of randomly drawn numbers. The numbers are called out until someone wins; a few veterans get up to 10 cards playing at once. No lessons required.

Blackjack (or 21)

This is the most popular live table game in Las Vegas – and the easiest card game to learn – due to its relative simplicity.

The luck of the Irish

The object is to play against the dealer (house) and draw cards as close to 21 as possible without 'busting' (going over 21). There are several optional bets – splitting, doubling down, insurance (never take insurance) – and variations that include single-deck vs. multi-deck card shoes, and hands dealt face-up (as opposed to one card down). The house advantage is that if you bust, the dealer takes your money even if he busts too.

Craps

This is the raucous game of cheering (and cursing) crowds, where everyone at the table has a stake in what one hapless gambler does with the dice. Loud players, dramatically placed chips, and flying dice all revolve around a set of complex betting rules, and the fact that 7 is more likely to be rolled than any other number. Bets are placed for and against the dice thrower (or 'shooter'). Money changes hands very quickly at a craps table, making it another candidate for lessons, and it's not as complicated as it looks. But don't even lean against a craps table unless you know what you're doing, or have plenty of money to lose.

An elegantly attired waitress at Caesars Palace

Keno

Another game similar to a lottery, keno is usually played sitting in a casino coffee

shop. Unlike bingo, however, the odds are shifted in
that players circle random
numbers on a purchased
ticket and wait for a fixed
set of numbers to be drawn.
It's easy to play: pick up to
15 numbers on the 80-num-
ber slip, then hand it and
your money (usually $1 per
game) to the keno runner,
and she'll return a computerized ticket. Watch the illuminated keno board above

Dice are made to an accuracy
of 1/10,000th of an inch

to see if enough of your numbers come up to win. The odds
of winning are very low – in fact, the house advantage is
greater than that of any other casino game – but it's an
inexpensive way to pass the time while you're eating.

Pai Gow

If you enjoy poker, gambling at a mild pace, and playing
against no house advantage, you'll love Pai Gow. Each player is dealt seven cards, which are then arranged by the player
into two piles: one five-card hand and one two-card hand.
Standard poker rules apply; that is, pairs, straights, flushes,
full houses, are ranked in a hierarchy of hands to determine
the winner. The five-card hand must beat the two-card hand,
and both hands must beat the dealer's two hands in order to
win. If only one of the dealer's hands wins, the game is a 'push'
(tie), and no money changes hands (this happens more often
than not). If both the dealer's hands win, you lose. It's perfectly
acceptable to ask the dealer for advice on how to play your
hand (and a great way to learn). The caveat is that since the
house has no advantage, it takes 5 percent of your winnings.

Poker

A high-stakes card game played in a high-pressure atmosphere. Unlike most other card games, gamblers here play against each other; the house operates the game for a fixed percentage of each pot, usually 5 percent. There are many variations on offer, from the standard 7-card stud to Texas Hold 'Em. If you're new to the game, this might be an expensive place to learn. If you are a poker regular, Las Vegas is a great place to play, but watch out. As the old poker adage goes, 'Sit at the table, and figure out who the fool is. If you still don't know after five minutes, get up and leave. It's bound to be you.'

Roulette

A subdued game of European flair, roulette is a relatively simple game, where bets are placed by laying chips on a single number or groups of numbers, colors, or even/odd. Different players are given different colored chips to avoid confusion. The wheel is spun, the ball drops, and where it lands determines the outcome. Odds are as high as 35 to 1, which means a single $5 chip on the right number wins $175. (Handy hint: avoid playing a double-zero wheel and search for those with only one zero.) Winning numbers are illuminated at each table to attract passers-by into thinking 'It's hitting my number!'

Slot Machines

Slot machines have become the most popular form of gaming in Las Vegas – so much so that they supersede the play at table games in many casinos. Though all modern slot machines are computerized, the rules are the same: get three or four matching icons in a row (or some combination thereof) and you win. The difference is that the computer decides when you win, not pure chance. And even though the payback increases the more you bet on a single pull, the computer will decrease your odds of winning. The skill, they say, is to find a slot machine that's 'hitting'; that is, a computer that's programmed to pay out big money.

Video Poker

Video poker has become increasingly popular, so much so that there's hardly a bar, grocery store, or laundromat in Las Vegas that doesn't have at least two or three machines. It's the same as regular five-card draw, with the machine acting as dealer. Unlike slots, interaction and a semblance of skill are required; that is, you are offered a choice on how to play the hand you're dealt. A chart on the screen lists the payoff of your winning hand and, as with slots, the more you bet, the better the payoff. Versions of video poker range from 'Jacks or Better' (the standard game) to 'Double Bonus' or 'Deuces Wild,' although the more wild cards involved, the lower the payoff. Some casinos now also offer video blackjack.

Playing the slots at the Sahara

Folies Bergères at the Tropicana is a Las Vegas classic

THE BIG SHOWS

Once, Las Vegas showrooms were filled with top-notch entertainment – headliners, comedians, production shows, and dancing girls – all at a very low price. In that bygone era, elaborate dinner shows were seen by the casinos as a loss leader, a way to keep customers happily dropping money at the tables or the slot machines. As long as the bottom line was glittering, the casino operators, especially during the days of the Mob, were happy to continue providing entertainment and food very inexpensively, or even for free.

When corporations moved in with more stringent departmental accounting procedures, every sector of a hotel-casino had to show success. Not satisfied with a simple overall profit, corporate operators began to both raise prices and cut corners, resulting in an era of frustrating mediocrity from which Las Vegas has only recently emerged.

Now, most showrooms are again offering quality stars and elaborate productions, *sans* the accompanying dinner service. Prices have certainly risen, but so has the benchmark of quality. Some of the bigger shows and headliner appearances (especially during major events like New Year's Eve) exceed over $100 per ticket – typical for New York, but previously unheard of in Las Vegas. What this means is that, in the case of showroom entertainers, the old adage of 'getting what you pay for' now applies to Las Vegas.

Keeping up with the Shows

Although the runs for the shows listed here are considered open-ended, remember that nothing is static in Las Vegas. Entire resorts open and close, and showrooms sometimes change show times, prices, or featured productions. Also, there are numerous headlining entertainers who change from week to week. For current listings of all the entertainment around town, pick up a copy of *Showbiz Weekly* or *What's On In Las Vegas*, the two most comprehensive listings guides. In the reviews below, 'dark' refers to the day when the show does not play at all. Please remember that it is an old tradition for showgirls in Las Vegas production shows to be topless and that tradition continues, so some of the shows listed here are not appropriate for children.

A Britney Spears impersonator at American Superstars

American Superstars: Of the cavalcade of impersonator shows, this one is skewed heavily toward the modern era. Talented performers provide energetic renditions

The innovative Blue Man Group's take on mime

of Madonna, Michael Jackson, Ricky Martin, and Christina Aguilera, among others. The *Las Vegas Advisor* has described this popular entertainment as the 'best value in town.' *Stratosphere Hotel and Casino, 2000 Las Vegas Boulevard South; tel: 702-380 7777. Shows 7pm Sunday–Tuesday; 6.30 and 8.30pm on Wednesday, Friday and Saturday; dark Thursday; (special rate for children 5–12 years of age).*

Blue Man Group: This award-winning show features three bald, blue characters. The one-of-a-kind showroom experience has been called innovative, hilarious, and musically powerful. *The Venetian, 3355 Las Vegas Boulevard South; tel: 702-987 2222. Shows 8pm Sunday–Friday; 7 and 10pm Saturday.*

Lance Burton – Master Magician: Set in a wonderful environment – an impeccably gilded theater that somehow maintains intimacy – magician Lance Burton pulls off extraordinary illusions with the assistance of a talented group of dancers. His residence is due to end in 2009. *Monte Carlo Hotel and Casino, 3770 Las Vegas Boulevard South; tel: 702-730 7777. Shows 7 and 10pm; dark Sunday and Monday.*

Cirque du Soleil's KÀ: The internationally famed Cirque applies the visual vocabulary of cinema to a dazzling live event that is all about storytelling. *MGM Grand, 3799 Las Vegas Boulevard South; tel: 702-891 7777. Shows 7.30 and 10.30, dark Sunday and Monday.*

Cirque du Soleil's Love: Originally conceived by the late George Harrison and his friend, Cirque founder Guy Laliberté, this celebration of the Beatles' songs features psychedelic lighting, rare and remastered music and, of course, amazing acrobatics. *Mirage, 3400 Las Vegas Boulevard South, tel: 702-791-7111. Shows 7pm and 10pm, dark Tuesday and Wednesday.*

Cirque du Soleil's Mystère: With this show traditional circus is taken to new levels of sophistication in an amazing state-of-the-art theater. No animals are used by the Cirque du Soleil, just 72 performers of amazing physical and emotive skill and grace. This popular show was the Cirque's first in Las Vegas. A unique experience that borders on performance art. *T.I. (Treasure Island), 3300 Las Vegas Boulevard South; tel: 702-894 7111. Shows 7.30 and 10.30pm; dark Monday and Tuesday.*

Cirque du Soleil's O: From the acclaimed international troupe, *O* dazzles audiences in an aquatic environment that utilizes about 1½ million gallons (6.8 million liters) of water. Around 75 highly skilled acrobats – all scuba-certified – dive, swim, and perform trapeze and high-wire acts in a remarkable auditorium. *Bellagio Hotel and Casino, 3600 Las*

Cirque du Soleil presents five different shows in Las Vegas

There's no business like show business!

Vegas Boulevard South; tel: 702-693 7111. Shows 7.30 and 11pm; dark Wednesday and Thursday.

Cirque du Soleil's Zumanity: The fine Canadian corps presents an adult-themed, erotic evening. Showcasing 'human sensuality, arousal, and eroticism,' with 50 performers, including acrobats, contortionists and magicians. *New York-New York Hotel and Casino, 3790 Las Vegas Boulevard South, tel: 702-740 6969. Shows 7.30pm and 10.30pm, Tuesday through Saturday.*

Folies Bergère: The Las Vegas home of the famous topless dancers since 1961, the Tropicana's show was recently revamped and updated. Nothing says 'Las Vegas' quite like this; the glittering costumes and chorus line of showgirls is what the myth is based on. *Tropicana Resort and Casino, 3801 Las Vegas Boulevard South; tel: 702-739 2222. Shows 7.30 and 10pm; dark Thursday.*

Danny Gans – The Man of Many Voices: What started as a short-lived Las Vegas stint at the Stratosphere Tower has evolved into one of the most popular shows in town. Gans is an amazing impersonator and an energetic showman who has mastered the art of entertainment. *Mirage Hotel and Casino, 7900 Las Vegas Boulevard South; tel: 702-791 7111. Shows 8pm; dark Monday and Friday.*

Jubilee!: Long before the blockbuster movie, *Jubilee!* was sinking the *Titanic* on the Strip in what is the show's amazing signature special effect. The production also features dozens of topless and costumed showgirls, making this an event – in true Las Vegas tradition – for adults only. *Bally's Hotel and Casino, 3645 Las Vegas Boulevard South; tel: 702-739 4111. Shows 7.30 and 10.30pm Saturday to Thursday; dark Friday.*

Legends In Concert: A strong favorite of many return visitors, this classic Las Vegas impersonation show features all the greats from yesterday and today. Impersonators render uncanny performances of the Four Tops and Elvis, as well as modern stars like Garth Brooks and Shania Twain. *Imperial Palace Hotel and Casino, 3535 Las Vegas Boulevard South; tel: 702-731 3311. Shows 7.30 and 10.30pm; dark Sunday.*

Barry Manilow: The 1970s crooner reprises his career, from his Brooklyn boyhood and Julliard education to recording, stage and TV stardom, in this musical self-portrait presented in a theater that Hilton built just for him. *Las Vegas Hilton, 3000 South Paradise Road, tel: 702-732 5111. Shows 8pm Wednesday–Saturday; dark Sunday–Tuesday.*

Bette Midler: The Divine Miss M headlines five nights a week at Caesars' Colosseum, right down the street from Barry Manilow, who started as her piano accompanist, playing New York's gay bathhouses more than 35 years ago. Replete with sequins and feather boas, the show is a fitting climax to a simply stunning career. Elton John's Red Piano show plays in the venue on some of Midler's nights off. *Caesars Palace, 3570 Las Vegas Boulevard South, tel: 702-731 7110. Shows 7.30 pm Friday to Sunday, Tuesday and Wednesday, dark Monday and Thursday.*

Monty Python's Spamalot: Adapted from the 1975 movie Monty Python and the Holy Grail by creator Eric Idol, the Tony-winning Broadway hit has been stripped down Vegas-style to a hilarious, fast-paced 90 minutes and beefed up with plenty of scantily clad wenches. *Wynn Las Vegas, 3131 Las Vegas Boulevard South; tel: 702-770 7100. Shows 8pm Sunday to Wednesday and Friday, 7pm and 10pm Saturday, dark Thursday.*

Penn & Teller: The dynamic magic duo entertain in their own theater in the Rio Hotel, performing new tricks, exposing how old ones are done, and generally being genial. *The Rio, 3700 W. Flamingo Road; tel: 702-252 7777. Shows 9pm Wednesday to Monday; dark Tuesday.*

Le Rêve: Subtitled 'a Small Collection of Imperfect Dreams,' this is a visually stunning journey into the world of sleep, set in and around a huge tank of water which serves as a stage. Note: visitors in the first three rows of the audience might get wet. *Wynn Las Vegas, 3131 Las Vegas Boulevard South; tel: 702-770 7100. Shows 7.30 and 10.30pm Saturday to Wednesday; dark Thursday and Friday.*

A medieval villain

Tournament of Kings: A classic dinner show and great fun for families: a recreation of a medieval knights' jousting tournament, with swooning maidens and fearsome dragons galore. *Excalibur Hotel and Casino, 3850 Las Vegas Boulevard South; tel: 702-597 76000. Shows 6 and 8.30pm; dark Tuesday.*

ADULT ENTERTAINMENT

For all the hype about Las Vegas's conversion to a family town, the truth is that beyond all the shiny big-name properties lies a bevy of adult-oriented distractions. In recent years efforts have been made to eliminate the seediest and most disreputable of these, while those operating within the law have flour-

The Riviera's famous 'crazy girls' statue

ished. As a result, Las Vegas seems ready to accept the multiple layers of complexity its status as a tourist city throws up.

Many of the resorts on the Strip have appeased family visitors by cleaning up their shows and covering up their showgirls. But at the **Riviera** most shows are adult-oriented; for raucous fun, choose *Crazy Girls* (it gets even more outrageous during convention season). There's also the long-running *Folies Bergères* at the **Tropicana**, now an institution.

The most popular 'topless' shows on the Strip today are girls'-night-out male stripper shows such as Chippendales at the **Rio** and Thunder from Down Under at the **Excalibur.**

There are dozens of clubs other than casinos that offer either nude or topless entertainment. Most of the topless-only clubs have full bars. For totally nude dancers, the choices are just as varied, but due to Vegas' complicated licensing laws, most do not serve alcohol. For both drinks and skin (male or female), try the **Spearmint Rhino**, 3344 Highland Drive, or **Cheetah's**, 2112 Western Avenue. **Girls of Glitter Gulch**, 20 East Fremont, is as historic as it is titillating, and the sexiest attraction in the Fremont Street Experience.

NIGHTLIFE

From local bars featuring live music and comedy to night-clubs, and music venues, the city's after-dusk life beyond gambling and shows is very healthy. For a detailed listing of local events beyond the Strip, pick up one of the two free alternative newsweeklies, *CityLife* or *Las Vegas Weekly*.

After the heady days of the 1950s, nightclubbing took a nose-dive but is popular again, thanks to a resurgence of dance music. This has led to a deluge of hotel-based high-energy clubs, including **LAX** in the Luxor, **Studio 54** in the MGM Grand and **Rain** in the Palms. The Palms is also home to **ghostbar**, which has to-die-for Vegas views and a glass floor looking way down into the pool. Each club caters to a specific crowd, so hunt around until you find the one for you.

Gay Clubs

Gays and lesbians can find much integrated nightlife in the so-called 'Fruit Loop' area on Paradise Road. But for years, **Gipsy,** 4605 Paradise Road, tel: 702-731 1919 has been the gay venue to beat: the most uninhibited and unpretentious dance club in town.

Music Venues

Vegas has live music venues to fit all gigs and budgets. Two local spots, where you are as likely to spy a real resident as you are an intrepid tourist sneaking away from the Strip, are the **Sam Boyd Stadium**, an outdoor venue for big-ticket acts, and the **Thomas and Mack Center** on the University of Nevada at Las Vegas campus, hosting music as well as sports events.

Never to be outdone, the big resorts also cater to music fans. The largest venue is the MGM Grand **Garden Arena,** modeled after New York City's Madison Square Garden. Home of the Billboard Music Awards, shows from the Garden starring Britney or Elton are likely to turn up on cable TV.

The popular Mandalay Bay **Events Center** showcases everyone from rock shows to opera stars, but arrive early to avoid the long entry lines. Large seats and spacious rows make the 9,000-seater **Orleans Arena** a very comfortable venue, or catch a Broadway show or recording artist at the **Theatre for the Performing Arts**. Two casino-based music venues that are as classy and hip as anywhere in the US are Mandalay Bay's **House of Blues**, where the Sunday gospel brunch is not to be missed, and the Hard Rock Casino's 1,400-seat **The Joint**, with probably the best sound system in the city. The newest large concert venue in town is **Pearl**, opened in 2007 at the Palms.

Live music Downtown

The Forum Shops – a vision from ancient Rome

SHOPPING

Where there is money, there is shopping, and shopping facilities have always been around in Vegas. But compared with other major cities, these facilities didn't live up to expectation. Hotel shopping areas consisted of retailers selling mostly expensive and tacky (or sometimes cheap and tacky) merchandise, and malls were nothing more than utilitarian outlets. In recent years, this scenario has changed dramatically.

As the city expands, so do the shopping facilities. Groups of stores are now marketed as 'retail destinations' and compete with the casinos in sound, light, and entertainment amenities. The Forum Shops (at Caesars Palace) started the trend, placing its outlets under an indoor 'sky' that changes color, simulating dawn to dusk several times a day. Desert Passage took this a step further: as well as an indoor 'rainstorm', the facades of its stores were beautifully landscaped, echoing the Arabian theme of its neighbor casino, the Aladdin. It is now home to the Miracle Mile shopping centre. Elegant hotel-based shopping promenades have also emerged at the Venetian and Bellagio resorts. The Fashion Show Mall, long resident on the Strip, recently increased its floor space, glitzed up its image with fashion shows and exhibitions and installed a gigantic outdoor 'cloud'.

There are two outlet malls within a short drive, and a few good local stores.

Shopping Malls

The **Forum Shops**, located at Caesars Palace casino, was the first themed indoor shopping promenade, built to look and feel like an outdoor Roman street. It surprised quite a few observers in 1992 by attracting not only the obvious tourists from the Strip, but also more than a handful of shopping-starved locals eager to explore stores they once had to travel out-of-state to visit. The number of restaurants and entertainment outlets made the Forum a great place for an all-day, one-stop spending spree, and fueled the trend for others.

Not to be left behind, resort-casinos decided their guests (and a novelty-seeking public) would enjoy having retail possibilities that matched the caliber of their hotels. As expected, upscale stores like Tiffany, Versace, and Prada dominate **Shopping le Boulevard** at Paris Las Vegas and **Via Bellagio** at Bellagio, while the **Grand Canal Shoppes** is a major part of the Venetian's centerpiece attraction. Wynn Las Vegas has a Ferrari-Maserati show-room on its premises, with more than a dozen examples of vehicles flaunting a $700,000+ price tag. Even though there's an admission fee, there's often a line of

Good for the sole

Walking the malls can be hard on the feet, just like the miles of casino aisles. For comfort, wear soft-soled shoes.

people waiting to enter, presumably dreaming of how to spend that big win at the gaming tables. The **Wynn Esplanade** contains suitably high-end stores.

Rivaling the Forum Shops in size, **Miracle Mile**, adjacent to Planet Hollywood, specializes in second locations of unique non-chain retail stores from around the US in a sleek setting that retains vestiges of the former Desert Passage mall.

The Fashion Show Mall is the largest shopping destination on the Strip, attracting good key stores such as Saks, Lord & Taylor, Macy's, and Nordstrom. The massive state-of-the-art Great Hall is used for fashion shows and product-launch events (including cars), and the signature architectural steel 'cloud' canopy rises 20 stories into the air, employed as a huge projection canvas during the evening.

The Galleria at Sunset is a recent suburban shopping mall, located in the upscale Green Valley area in the nearby town of Henderson. Across from the Sunset Station Hotel and Casino, the mall houses a selection of interesting specialty stores in addition to department stores and a massive food court.

Factory Outlet Malls

Not far away from the Strip (although you will need a car or taxi) is **Las Vegas Outlets**, an indoor mall with 145 stores, bargain opportunities ranging from clothing to electronics.

On the way to Downtown, **Las Vegas Premium Outlets**, offers 435,000 square feet (40,000 sq m) of shopping in an upscale, village setting, located just off Interstate 15 and Charleston Boulevard.

The **Fashion Outlets of Las Vegas** at Primm, Nevada (on the California state line) is one of the best of the outlet malls. It's a 30-minute drive away on Interstate 15 (or a several-times-daily shuttle bus from New York-New York; tel: 1-888-424 6898), but the selection of top names (Versace, Tommy Hilfiger) and specialty stores make it worth the trip.

Local Shopping

Beyond the malls lie hundreds of unique specialty stores. From ethnic food and vintage clothing stores to electronics and book stores, there are many interesting shopping spots that escape the attention of most tourists. Here are a few highlights; for the names of more specialty stores, pick up one of the city's free newsweeklies, *CityLife* or *Las Vegas Weekly*.

The Attic, tel: 702-388 4088, may be the most famous vintage store in America, owing to it featuring in both a Visa credit-card commercial and on extreme sports TV network ESPN II. This two-story collection of clothes, appliances, and knick-knacks serves a willing audience with its selection of period clothing, often being called upon to provide items for movies being filmed in Las Vegas. Plan on spending a long time at this store, which is located at 1018 South Main Street.

Miracle Mile brings the outdoors indoors

Anyone who wears glasses will appreciate the Strip location of **Optica of Las Vegas**, tel: 702-735 8557, a full service optometry store that repairs eyewear, provides exams, and sets visitors up with a new set of prescription glasses or contact lenses – all within a couple of days. The designer-frame selection is among the best in town.

For souvenirs of the innately Las Vegas kind, there is the **Gamblers' General Store**, tel: 702-382 9903, a centrally located supplier of slot machines, gaming tables, and other gaming accoutrements large and small. Most items can be shipped for the purchaser if requested.

Las Vegas is one of the few North American cities that doesn't frown on smokers. For a taste of authentic Native American tobacco, the **Paiute Tribal Smoke Shop**, tel: 702-387 6433 sells tax-free tobacco products from its drive-through window, so you can cruise right back to the casino, light up, and lose all that money you just saved.

Weddings

Getting married almost ranks as a sport in Las Vegas, America's favorite city in which to tie the knot. More than 100,000 couples take the plunge here every year. Dozens of celebrities, including Michael Jordan, Elvis Presley, Britney Spears, and Richard Gere, have exchanged vows in Vegas; many of the chapels on Las Vegas Boulevard and Main Street have signs boasting of the big names they've joined in matrimony.

Most weddings are anything but traditional. You can use the drive-up wedding window at Chapel by the Courthouse (tel: 702-384 9099), have an Elvis impersonator sing your nuptials at the Graceland Wedding Chapel (tel: 702-474 6655), or get married in a helicopter over the Strip. Other options range from a bungee-jumping ceremony to saying your vows on a boat on Lake Mead. Theme weddings – with everyone dressed in 'Star Trek' suits or medieval costume – have also become popular.

SPORTS

Las Vegas is a sporting city. Whether you want to watch championship boxing matches, bet on the New York Giants, go paragliding, skiing, or play 18 holes of golf, all it takes is the right toys and/or plenty of cash. If you engage in an outdoor sport, though, remember that valley temperatures can reach well above 100°F (38°C) in summer and below freezing in winter, so it's very important to follow any local precautions, like using sunscreen or buying thermal underwear.

The Vegas area has many good golf courses

Spectator Sports
Boxing

Las Vegas has a long boxing history, having hosted enough championship fights to qualify as a capital of the sport. A big-time bout at one of the three resorts that handle most of the action – the MGM Grand, Caesars Palace, or the Mirage – invariably draws a crowd heavy on celebrities.

Golf Tournaments

The Las Vegas Invitational held every fall – known as the first professional tournament for famed champion Tiger Woods in 1996 – is considered the city's top golf attraction. At least three courses split the action, including the Tournament Players Club at the Canyons, while the home course

The Las Vegas Motor Speedway

and all weekend play is at the TPC at Summerlin. The well-watered greens around the city are also home to the Las Vegas Senior Classic every spring, and a draw for golf's big names. Check out the PGA website at <www.pgatour.com> for up-to-date information, and other local golfing events.

Bowling

Las Vegas has always had an affinity for bowling. The PBA holds both national and senior televised tournaments here at the Showboat Bowling Center in January.

Motor Sports

Serious racing arrived in Vegas in 1996 with the opening of the Las Vegas Motor Speedway, 17 miles (27km) north of Downtown on Interstate 15. The 1,500-acre (607-hectare) site is a speed-freak's dream: a 1½-mile (2.5-km) tri-oval super speedway, plus smaller clay and paved ovals, a drag strip, a road track, and a motocross course. Fans fill the 107,000-seat facility for NASCAR events like the Las Vegas 300, Winston West, and Craftsman Truck races, as well as the IRL Las Vegas 500.

The National Finals Rodeo

Held every December, this is the largest rodeo event in the country. It's an action-packed 10-day festival of the nation's top cowboys and cowgirls riding bulls, busting broncos, and roping calves at the Thomas and Mack Center. The city goes Western with endless satellite events, like beauty pageants, parties and dances at bars, cowboy-themed art exhibits, musical events at the Fremont Street Experience, and golf tournaments. If you want to attend, plan well ahead, as last-minute tickets for the big rodeo events are hard to come by.

Other Sports

While lacking a major sports franchise, Las Vegas is home to a triple-A baseball team and a Minor-League hockey squad. The Las Vegas Stars – the city's longest-running professional sports outfit – is a farm team for baseball's San Diego Padres; tickets are usually available for the Cashman Field home games. The Las Vegas Thunder hockey team (which is not affiliated with any NHL franchise) competes in the Thomas and Mack Center. During football and basketball seasons, the University of Nevada-Las Vegas fields teams in both sports. UNLV's basketball team has a storied history, winning the NCAA title in 1990.

Participatory Sports
Cycling

Avoid putting your mettle to the peddle on Sin City's busier streets; bicycle paths are few and courteous drivers even fewer. The best places are local parks or cycle-friendly spots beyond the city limits. One favorite, the 13-mile (21-km) scenic loop at Red Rock Canyon *(see page 65)*, explores some of the area's more picturesque landscapes and is not overly taxing.

Mountain bikers can call Escape Adventures, tel: 702-596 2953, to arrange a more rugged ride through the canyon's Cottonwood Valley. Another good bet: Floyd Lamb State Park, a few miles north on US95. These bike paths wind among ponds, trees, and historic buildings.

Golf

For a desert city, Las Vegas has more than enough grass fairways and water hazards to keep the most avid duffer busy – at least 70 courses in total. Guests staying at The Mirage, MGM Grand, Bellagio, T.I., the Golden Nugget, or New-York, New-York can play the spectacular Shadow Creek course, tel: 702-791 7161, for only $500 a time, limo included. Angel Park Golf Club, tel: 702-254 4653 is a municipal course with two 18-hole courses designed by Arnold Palmer, and Cloud Nine, a 12-hole par-3 course featuring replicas of famous par-3 holes from around the world.

The Las Vegas Paiute Resort, tel: 702-658 1400 is 20 miles (32km) north of town but well worth the trip: one of its two courses – called Snow Mountain – was once designated the best public course in Southern Nevada by *Golf Digest*. The Legacy Golf Club, tel: 702-897 2200, in Henderson is also well respected. For a locator map and a course-by-course description, go to <www.lasvegasgolf.com>.

Hiking

The Las Vegas Valley is rimmed with quality hiking trails. One of the more scenic is the 5-mile (8-km) River Mountain Trail with fine views of Lake Mead and the valley. Red Rock Canyon affords numerous routes, including a 2-mile (3-km) Pine Creek Canyon trek and a slightly longer walk along the attractive Keystone Thrust Trail. Mount Charleston is webbed with good

Nevada's hills are perfect for mountain biking

hikes; the ranger station can supply information, tel: 702-873 8800. Another fine spot is the Valley of Fire *(see page 64)*.

Rock Climbing

Red Rock Canyon, just 20 minutes from the Strip, has the best climbing in the region. There are literally thousands of challenges, from small bouldering routes to towering, experts-only cliffs. Spring and fall are the best seasons, but on almost any weekend there will be a cross-section of the international rock-jock community roping up in the canyon. Sky's the Limit guide service, tel: 702-363 4533 can arrange climbing trips.

Snow Sports

Mount Charleston has a ski area, the Las Vegas Ski and Snowboard Resort, also known as Lee Canyon, tel: 702-385 2754. It has bunny, intermediate, and expert routes, along with ski rental, ski school, and a lounge. The natur-

al snowfall is often augmented by snow-making equipment. The resort has nine long runs on 40 acres (16 hectares), but despite its name, snowboarding is allowed only at certain times.

Tennis

Most resorts have tennis facilities, but these are often for guests only. Otherwise, the Spanish Oaks Tennis Club, tel: 702-876 5836, a membership sporting club, makes its courts available to non-members as well. The main municipal tennis courts are at the Amanda and Stacy Darling Memorial Tennis Center, tel: 702-229 2100.

The scary Big Shot is not for the faint hearted

LAS VEGAS FOR CHILDREN

Although Las Vegas is now an adult town again after a decade of wooing the family market, there are still a number of kid-friendly activities. Most casinos have at least some kind of arcade, but the true high-scorer is **GameWorks** next to the MGM Grand, with 47,000 sq ft (4,371 sq m) of games (more than 250) from traditional pin-ball outposts to high-tech diversions. If you play up an appetite, GameWorks also has a full-service restaurant, snack bar, and Starbucks Coffee outlet. Adults can relax in the bar and shoot pool while the kiddies shoot the arcade games.

In the Showcase Mall next to the MGM Grand and not far from GameWorks is **M&M World**, four stories of merchandise and memorabilia dedicated to the famous small, round and ever-popular candies. Inside, the miles of aisles are loaded with thousands of fun M&M-related knickknacks, souvenirs, and collectibles; for sheer novelty, sample the hard-to-find silver M&Ms.

For something with a little more educational value, take young kids to the **Lied Discovery Children's Museum** *(see page 59)*. The museum is full of interactive exhibits, including boots that let you feel what it is like to walk on another planet and a machine that shows how sand dunes form.

Thrills and Spills for Older Kids

Circus Circus' **Adventuredome**, a climate-controlled pink dome behind the venerable hotel-casino, boasts attractions including the Canyon Blaster corkscrew roller coaster, a water ride, bumper cars, carnival games, and a laser tag arena. The casino itself features kid-friendly free circus acts from 11am to midnight daily.

Roller-coaster aficionados will love the twisting, looping **Manhattan Express roller coaster** at New York-New York.

Casinos and Kids

By law, people under the age of 21 are not permitted in any casino gaming areas, bars, or lounges, but some casinos are child-friendly if certain rules are followed (children must not be left unattended; children may walk through a casino when accompanied by a parent but may not stop). Other casinos ban strollers from the premises or close the doors entirely to anyone under 18 unless they are guests staying with an adult. If you are a parent desperate for a little grown-up fun, however, most hotels can arrange babysitting services.

Once inside the hotel, stop at the extensive Coney Island-themed arcade. Ultra high-altitude thrills are the order of the day at the Stratosphere Tower. The **Big Shot** slingshot ride heightens the sensation of sudden vertical acceleration with its setting 1,100ft (335m) above the city, while **X-Scream** takes riders with stomachs of iron almost as high, then dangles them in the air. The **High Roller roller coaster** is atop the Strat Tower, too, but experienced riders consider the attraction too slow and uneventful, despite its giddying altitude.

Add a little zoom to your kids' day at the Sahara's **Cyber Speedway**, a huge (40,000-sq-ft/3,720-sq-m) playground of virtual reality auto racing in life-size NASCAR race cars, dozens of interactive rides, and two 3-D theaters.

Further Afield

Even farther from the bright lights is **Bonnie Springs-Old Nevada**, tel: 702-875 4191, a mock ghost town near Red Rock Canyon. The Wild-West town comes complete with gunfights, a wax museum, an opera house, a mini-train, horseback riding, and an extensive petting zoo.

Exploring the Lied Discovery Children's Museum

For motorized thrills, the **Las Vegas Mini Grand Prix**, tel: 702-259 7000, has the West's only banked-oval stock car track. Along with go-karts and kiddie karts, the 7-acre (3-hectare) facility provides wheels for big drivers, too.

Northwest of Henderson is the factory of **Ethel M. Chocolates**, tel: 888-627 0990, where self-guided tours are available every day.

Calendar of Events

January *The Super Bowl:* The biggest sports-betting day of the year; Sports Books are packed with anxious betters watching the game on giant-screen televisions. *PBA Classic:* A major stop on the Pro Bowlers tour. *Adult Entertainment Expo:* A four-day adult entertainment trade show held annually at the Sands Expo Center, embracing business, stars and lots of very enthusiastic fans.

February *Chinese New Year:* The biggest gambling day of the year. *Las Vegas International Marathon:* Really only a half marathon, but who could pass up the opportunity to run from Jean, Nevada, to the Strip on the old LA Highway? *Las Vegas Fun Fly:* A three-day event attracting the brightest and the best designers and fans of radio-controlled model aircraft.

May *Pride Week:* This city-sanctioned week of parades and parties celebrates Las Vegas's gay and lesbian community.

June *Helldorado Days:* A four-day rodeo, plus western parties and pageants celebrating Southern Nevada's cowpoke roots.

September *Las Vegas 500K IRL Race and NASCAR Craftsman Truck Series:* In one of the biggest weekend racing combinations in the US, these two races have been scheduled on the same weekend at the end of September since 1999.

October *PGA Las Vegas Invitational:* This four-day, internationally televised golf tournament from the Tournament Players Club in Summerlin and The Canyons is a major event on the world's golfing calendar.

November *COMDEX:* When the consumer-electronics industry descends on Las Vegas, geek world comes to town, meaning the streets are packed with traffic, hotel rooms are booked, and topless bars are crammed with revelers waving $1 bills.

December *CineVegas:* The premiere four-day film festival in Las Vegas always features a strong showing of unreleased films, festival winners, independents, and classics. *New Year's Eve:* Celebrate with 200,000 or more of your newest friends. Las Vegas's celebrations and the two major block parties that accompany them are challenging Times Square for attendees. Make your reservations early and come prepared to party.

EATING OUT

Dining in Las Vegas has been transformed. The wall-to-wall all-you-can-eat buffets have been sidelined, the celebrity chefs are here, and the standards and the stakes (steaks) have been raised all round. Although the high-ticket gastrodomes may not be perfect for every meal, they have definitely raised the culinary game. Prices in these eateries have nearly caught up with their New York, LA and San Franciscan cousins, but so, too, has the food and the service.

Catering at the more down-to-earth kitchens has become more expensive too, but the food is a lot better than the curling buffet fare of old. Sitting side-by-side with the paying customers are a new breed. Gamblers are regularly rewarded for their play by pit bosses scribbling out 'comps' (complimentary tickets) for the hotel's on-site restaurants. The level of the comp depends upon the level of play, so everyone – low-rollers to big spenders – can be accommodated. And what could be better than a free meal in Las Vegas?

Fanning the flames at a Vegas steak house

Cuisines of the World

With the arrival of Wolfgang Puck's Spago in 1992, the city began a slow but sure ascent from the depths of continental cuisine into the modern world of the nouvelle, haute, California, Pan Asian, and Pacific Rim. Since then, more 'name' chefs have brought their operations to Las Vegas, among them Emeril Lagasse and Jean-Louis Palladin.

Carnivores can't go wrong in Vegas

New on the Menu

Acting in concert with these arrivals was the hotels' new-found willingness to relinquish ownership and management of some of their dining spaces to experienced restaurateurs. The result for food lovers has been terrific. The improvement of the dining experience and the resulting rise of expectations led to an across-the-board renewal. Today, some of the city's – and even the country's – best restaurants are ensconced within hotel casinos, such as Picasso at Bellagio, Zeffirino at the Venetian, the Daniel Boulud Brasserie at Wynn Las Vegas, and Aureole at Mandalay Bay.

Bountiful Buffets

Despite these changes to the culinary landscape, buffets can still be a hit-and-miss affair, with many offering similar selections of prime rib, starchy vegetables, limp salads, and boring desserts. Others offer a wide array of cuisines – Mexican, Italian, American heartland (in other words, meat and potatoes), and vegetables – plus all the seconds, thirds, and fourths you can gulp down. The tantalizing buffets of lore – where the food is imaginatively selected and the prices low – do exist, but it may require searching them out.

The Rio's Carnival World Buffet is definitely a cut above, as is Main Street Station's Garden Court Buffet. But it and the worthwhile The Buffet at the Gold Nugget are no longer rock-bottom cheap, and all buffets, regardless of class, status, price, or time of day or night, have lines that stretch around the block.

Champagne Brunch

Sunday champagne brunches were once the best of the buffets, despite champagne that was not always palatable. Today, most are simply a more expensive version of the standard breakfast-lunch offerings. Bally's Sterling Brunch is a notable exception. Replete with ice sculptures, and fresh flowers, it is a spread fit for a king, but it is also expensive.

Theme restaurants have proliferated in Las Vegas. Local versions of the Hard Rock Cafe and the Harley Davidson Cafe

Celebrity Chefs

Wolfgang Puck started it all in 1992, when he opened a second location of his ultra chic Hollywood restaurant, Spago, in Caesars Palace. Six years later, hotelier Steve Wynn set the standard for casino resorts by hiring three of America's top chefs, Michael Mina, Todd English, and Jean-George Vongerichten, to run restaurants in the Bellagio. Today, every major resort has at least one extravagant restaurant where you need reservations weeks in advance. Award-winning chefs often follow Puck's tradition, naming their restaurants after themselves. You'll find David Burke in the Venetian, Bradley Ogden in Caesars, Emeril's in the MGM Grand, and as for Wolfgang Puck, he now has five restaurants on the Las Vegas Strip.

pull the same surprisingly brisk business that they do around the globe. Chain franchises from fast food to pancake houses are now sucking up much of the local dining budget. But when the population of Vegas skyrocketed in the middle of the last decade, more upscale chains also made their way to the valley. For a town starved of choice, this was manna from heaven. As a result, locally owned dining is also experiencing a boom, and many ethnic and specialty restaurants have opened.

Home-Grown Talent

One of the traditional areas of any major tourist city – a

Fine dining in Wolfgang Puck's restaurant in Caesars Palace

so-called restaurant row – has evolved piecemeal along Paradise Road, adding to the options. Here, diners can choose from a plethora of major restaurants, locally-owned eateries, plus some small tasty ethnic cafes, all within walking distance of each another. Chinatown, near Spring Mountain Road, is another good place to check out, offering excellent cuisine that includes Filipino and Vietnamese as well as the more traditional Chinese.

In fact, considering how rapidly the dining situation has improved – and the truckloads of money being spent to lure world-class chefs – Las Vegas may someday overtake all of its American rivals in the culinary sweepstakes.

HANDY TRAVEL TIPS

An A–Z Summary of Practical Information

A

ACCOMMODATIONS (See also CAMPING, YOUTH HOSTELS, and the list of RECOMMENDED HOTELS starting on page 125)

Las Vegas is a unique city in that the vast majority of its hotels offer both accommodations and attractions. Most of the places travelers want to see are found along the Strip or Downtown, so staying in one of these areas will put you right in the center of the action.

The quality of accommodations ranges from the best to the sleaziest, but most of the **hotel-casinos** fall comfortably into the average to above-average categories. Off-Strip hotel-casinos offer many of the same amenities – and sometimes more – as on-Strip hotels, and often at a lower price. Neighborhood hotel-casinos usually offer less in the way of amenities, but make up for it in price.

There are **non-gaming resorts** (such as the Four Seasons) if you prefer classy accommodations away from the clang of slot machines. Also, there are **non-gaming motels** all over the city, in the suburbs, and along Boulder Highway. Many of them specialize in extended stays of a week or more, and can be very good alternatives for travelers on a budget.

If you will be without a car, choose a hotel as close to your preferred action as possible. Las Vegas is spread widely, taxis are costly, and public transportation is still getting up to speed.

As there is no truly slow season in Las Vegas, room reservations are strongly advised, especially during the heavy travel periods in fall and spring and on any weekend, during major sporting events, for New Year's Eve, and whenever there is a major trade convention in town. In fact, some of the conventions draw over 200,000 people – enough to fill almost every room in the city. The **Las Vegas Convention and Visitors Authority**, tel: 702-892 0711, can alert you to when the events are in town. Alternatively, search the LVCVA website at **<www.visitlasvegas.com>** for availability, or visit another Vegas website like **<www.vegas.com>**.

There are still periods of relative quiet when rates are down and it is easier to find a room without reservations. The city is usually slower between Thanksgiving (fourth Thursday of November) and Christmas, as well as during the high-heat months of July and August. Then, room rates are up for grabs, and incredible bargains are to be had. If you're feeling brave-hearted, it's always worth negotiating on-the-spot and face-to-face. You could, for example, book a room on-line for the first couple of nights, then simply stroll from one resort to the next, asking for the best rate on that particular day.

AIRPORT

Las Vegas is served by one major airport, **McCarran International** (tel: 702-261 5211). With the growth in travel to Las Vegas, the airport is among the country's busiest, and recently added 26 gates to handle the flow. The airport is also very close to town, within a 15-minute drive of Tropicana Avenue and the Strip. Transportation to and from the airport is available via an unending stream of taxis.

For a cheaper ride, try one of the shuttle buses that operate 24 hours and take you directly to your hotel. One such company is **Bell Trans** (tel: 702-739 7990). A public bus also serves the airport, but it takes far longer than the relatively inexpensive shuttle buses. Plans are underway to extend the Strip monorail to the airport.

B

BICYCLE RENTAL

Bicycle riding within the city is not advised. For bicycle rental and tours of the surrounding natural areas by bicycle, call **Escape Adventures** on 702-596 2953.

BUDGETING FOR YOUR TRIP

Las Vegas is one of the less expensive vacation destinations in the US – if you stay away from the tables. Once a flight has been paid for, everything else can be done on the cheap, from dining at a $7.99 all-you-can-eat buffet, to staying in a decent motel for as little as $25 per night. Sin City is a place that likes to do deals, and car rental firms and even major casinos often offer astonishingly low prices, usually in the hot summer months of July and August. If money is tight, it's worth deciding in advance when you want to go, and shopping around on the web for competitive offers. Of course, it's also possible to spend a fortune in Vegas, especially if you take advantage of all the shopping and show opportunities; top shows like Cirque du Soleil can cost up to $150 per ticket. Museums and attractions charge hefty admission prices, too, often around $20.

But the best way to lose money is to gamble. Setting and holding yourself to a budget is an important part of any trip to Las Vegas. Decide before leaving home exactly how much per day you have for gambling and do not permit yourself to exceed that amount; access to bank accounts via ATM cards is far too easy, and many only dole out $100s. More than a few travelers have arrived here happy, only to be forced to sell a prized possession for the fare home.

Tipping must be budgeted for as well. It is a recognized and accepted part of Las Vegas culture, and being unprepared can result in poor service (see TIPPING).

C

CAMPING

Within the city limits, there are plenty of RV parks, as well as a **KOA** (tel: 702-733 9707) on Boulder Highway that has both RV and the only in-town tent sites. Other parks include those at Sam's Town and the Showboat, both on Boulder Highway.

Outside of the city, camping is plentiful in Red Rock Canyon, the Valley of Fire, and Mount Charleston, with Red Rock being only 30 minutes from the city (see Excursions, page 64).

CAR RENTAL

Visitors who want any degree of freedom rent cars, and most do so at the airport on arrival. Advance reservations are suggested but not required. The local telephone directory lists 17 pages of rental agencies, all of the major US companies being represented (Alamo, Avis, Budget, Dollar, Enterprise, Hertz, National, and Thrifty), and rates are generally below the US average. The major companies usually won't rent to drivers under 25 years old, but some of the local companies will. All rental companies require a driver's license and a major credit card matching the license. Price quotes do not include taxes or liability and collision damage waivers (CDW). These can double the cost, so check with your credit card company to see what is already covered. No added insurance is required, but renters should weigh that choice carefully, since the heavy Las Vegas traffic is aggressive.

CLIMATE

Las Vegas is a desert region, making summer temperatures very warm and dry and winters cold. August temperatures can reach over 115°F (46°C) in the mid-afternoon, and still hover around 100°F (38°C) at midnight. Winter temperatures can be surprisingly brisk, dipping very quickly after the sun sets. Spring is warmer but windy; fall is often the best time to visit, with warm days and mild nights. The sun shines an average of 310 days per year, so bring sunglasses and leave the umbrella at home.

	J	F	M	A	M	J	J	A	S	O	N	D
High												
°F	47	50	55	63	73	83	90	87	80	67	53	45
°C	8	10	13	17	23	28	32	31	27	19	17	7
Low												
°F	33	37	42	49	59	68	75	73	65	53	41	33
°C	0	3	6	9	15	20	24	23	18	17	7	0

CLOTHING

Requirements for dressing in Las Vegas have fluctuated over the years, from the formality of the 1940s through the 1960s to the T-shirts and shorts of the 1990s. Today's styles range from upscale sumptuous to downright shoddy, with everything imaginable in between. Little is out of place here, though remember that many of the better restaurants require jackets and ties for men.

Remember also to pack clothing appropriate for the weather; short sleeves and skirts or shorts are accepted and nearly required for spending time outside in the summer months. Heavy winter jackets are what most winter visitors forget to pack, not expecting the chill of the winds that frequently assail the city. Sunblock is a must; a style-appropriate hat, or at least a pair of sunglasses, is highly recommended.

CRIME AND SAFETY

Las Vegas is a fairly safe place considering the high volume of tourist traffic with which it must contend. Hotel security is notoriously efficient (look up; the black-glass bubbles on the ceilings are a marker of security cameras monitored 24 hours a day), and Metro police bicycle patrols help curb problems along the Strip and Downtown. Still, standard big-city precautions should be taken. Avoid dark areas, especially Downtown. Pick-pocketing on city buses and in crowded areas – such as the Treasure Island pirate show or Bellagio's fountain display – is notorious, so watch your suitcases, purse, or wallet. In any emergency, dial 911 from any phone; no coins needed.

But visitors are much more likely to become a victim of an accident than they are a crime. Tourists walking down the Strip often become distracted by all the visual stimuli, so much so that in one two-year period, 134 pedestrians were killed by motorists. In many cases, the pedestrians were at fault, meandering into streets while looking at the lights, foolishly crossing the Strip's eight lanes of bumper-to-bumper traffic between lights, or simply backing into a lane of traffic while angling for a photograph. When walking in Las

Vegas it is crucial to remember that, despite the temptation, you must not jaywalk or hop over barricades meant to prohibit pedestrian travel; otherwise you may be fined. Motorists are notoriously possessive of their travel lanes, and laws are set against pedestrians that violate the travel lane beyond a crosswalk.

CUSTOMS AND ENTRY FORMALITIES

All international visitors need passports. Citizens of Canada, Mexico, and most western European nations, as well as Australia, New Zealand, and Japan, can stay for up to 90 days without a visa, as long as they have a valid passport and a return air ticket. Others entering the US might need visas. Security arrangements since September 11, 2001, mean it's a good idea to carry proof of identity wherever you go.

Adult visitors staying longer than 72 hours may bring along the following items duty free: 1 liter of wine or liquor; 100 cigars (non-Cuban), or 3lbs (1.5kg) of tobacco, or 200 cigarettes (though they are so cheap here, one wonders why); and gifts valued under $100. Absolutely no food (including canned goods) or plants of any type are permissible. Visitors may also arrive and depart with up to $10,000 currency without declaration.

D

DRIVING

Driving can be a difficult experience for anyone unused to city traffic. Las Vegas streets are busy and the drivers aggressive and unpredictable. Roads that are complete are in very good condition, owing to recent widening and paving. But there are many roadways under perpetual expansion and construction, making every day a new and frustrating experience.

A right turn on a red light is permitted in Vegas, unless otherwise posted, as are most U-turns. When a stoplight turns green, be sure to check both directions before proceeding; Las Vegans are notorious for their attempts (and failures) to beat the traffic signal. Watch for school-crossing zones; fines are high and local patrols are often on watch. However tempting, never drink and drive, as penalties are stiff and can include an immediate period in jail.

Freeways are the I-15 traveling north from Los Angeles to Salt Lake City, and US93/95, which comes from Arizona toward Utah. The new Interstate 215 freeway connects the Strip and airport with the booming suburb of Henderson,

Parking is easy, with every hotel offering free parking lots or structures (Downtown requires a casino cage validation). Valet parking is a free at-the-door service, but tips are customary. Remember that on busy nights, the valet may take longer to retrieve your car than you could have if you parked yourself (see TIPPING).

Gasoline is plentiful, available on nearly every corner and, though expensive by US standards, inexpensive compared to elsewhere in the world, especially Europe.

E

ELECTRIC CURRENT

All of the United States uses a 110-120 volt 50-cycle alternating current (AC). Transformers or plug adaptors are required for appliances using any other voltage, and are widely available.

EMERGENCIES

Dial **911** from any phone, toll-free.

G

GAY AND LESBIAN TRAVELERS

While Las Vegas may have a reputation as Sin City, it is only quietly tolerant of its fairly large gay and lesbian community, in the same look-the-other-way manner in which many gay entertainers have been accepted. Many gay businesses, bars, and nightclubs are centered in the small, energetic 'Fruit Loop', an area off Paradise Road between Harmon and Tropicana. For information and good listings, pick up *Q-Vegas* magazine, available at most major record and bookstores.

GETTING THERE (see also AIRPORT and DRIVING)

There are only three modern methods of transportation available for passengers coming to Las Vegas: air, bus, or car, though there are plans to begin casino-sponsored train service from Los Angeles, which would arrive at the Downtown train station.

By air. Las Vegas, though a major travel destination, is still considered a second-tier city when it comes to direct flights. While most major US cities, especially in the West, offer direct flights into McCarran International (the city's only major airport), many East Coast cities use hubs such as Denver, Chicago, and Phoenix. While some airlines add new direct flights on occasion, others withdraw theirs.

Direct, international flights come from Tokyo, Frankfurt, and London. Call the **Las Vegas Convention and Visitors Authority** at 702-892 0711 for information about international direct flights; call your airline regarding other flights.

By bus. Greyhound Bus Lines offers daily bus travel to and from Las Vegas and surrounding cities. Call 1-800-231 2222 (toll-free in the US) for information.

GUIDES AND TOURS

Numerous tour operators are located in Las Vegas, and their advertisements can be found in almost every free guide available along the Strip, in addition to in hotel rooms. The majority specialize in tours of Southern Nevada's Lake Mead (where you can also take a high-speed boat or a dinner cruise); to Hoover Dam and Boulder City; or to Red Rock Canyon. One of the most exciting excursions, which can be done by bus, plane, or mostly glamorously of all, by helicopter, is to the Grand Canyon *(see page 66)*. This return-trip journey can be done in under a day, returning to Sin City just in time to have a shower, a late dinner and hit the casinos that same evening.

H

HEALTH AND MEDICAL CARE

Las Vegas is a modern city with modern health care and food standards. In the event of an emergency, there are seven area hospitals that provide 24-hour emergency care. Travelers needing medical attention in a non-emergency situation should seek out one of the **University Medical Center Quick Care** clinics (tel: 702-383 2000), which has several locations in the Vegas vicinity; go to: <www.umcsn.com/quickcares> for a map. These centers require no appointments, and accept most patients, but be prepared to wait up to an hour or two. If you have no health insurance (or insurance is not recognized), you will have to pay for medical services immediately, so be sure to ask in advance about payment procedures.

Complementing this, there are several pharmacies for prescription and non-prescription drugs. **Walgreens** has over a dozen locations; most are open 24 hours daily.

HOLIDAYS

Most businesses' opening hours are similar to public holidays. Hotel-casinos and resorts never close, regardless of the day or time, but grocery stores keep shorter hours on Christmas and Thanksgiving (fourth Thursday of November). Government offices, schools, the post office, and banks are closed for 11 national holidays. Holiday times are extremely busy at Las Vegas airport. The Fourth of July and Thanksgiving holidays really attract the crowds, with Christmas following closely behind. Though not an official holiday in the US, Chinese New Year is the busiest holiday in Las Vegas casinos.

M

MEDIA

Las Vegas has two daily **newspapers**: the *Review-Journal* and the *Sun*. The *Review-Journal* has a more national orientation, while the *Sun* reads like the local metropolitan daily that it has always been. Hotel newsstands carry both, as well as the *New York Times, Los Angeles Times, USA Today,* and *Wall Street Journal.* For international newspapers, try Borders Bookshop, which has two locations.

There are a dozen **free local tourist guides**, ranging from small booklets of ads to more elaborate magazines with information content and listings. Two are *What's On* and *Las Vegas Magazine. What's On* is available in most hotel lobbies and on news racks, while the magazine is found in hotel rooms throughout the city.

Las Vegas also has two **free alternative newsweeklies**, *CityLife* and the *Las Vegas Weekly.* They are available citywide in coffeehouses, cafes, bookstores, clubs, bars, and newspaper racks, and contain extensive listings of off-Strip information.

The valley's **television** is primarily served by Cox Communications cable system, with almost 100 channels. Most hotel rooms have at least these stations: CNN, MTV, and USA networks, plus local affiliates ABC (channel 13), CBS (channel 8), FOX (channel 5), NBC (channel 3), and PBS (channel 10), though even the best hotels may not offer premium channels such as HBO – they'd prefer you to gamble rather than watch TV.

Radio has a full dial on both AM and FM bands. Highlights are KNPR (89.5FM, classical and NPR news), KUNV (91.5FM, jazz), KOMP (92.3FM, rock), KWNR (95.5FM, country-western), KXPT (97.1FM, classic and soft rock); KXTE (107.5FM, alternative rock), KDWN (720AM, talk), and KNUU (970AM, news).

MONEY MATTERS

Currency. The monetary unit in the US, the dollar, is based on the decimal system, with 100 cents per dollar. The United States is converting its well-known paper currency to a bold new design, but compared to the old, it appears almost fake. If you aren't sure, ask a casino cage.

Common banknotes are in the $1, $5, $10, $20, $50, and $100 denominations. If you are unfamiliar with dollars, be careful handling them. The bills are all the same size and color, and the denominations can be hard to distinguish in low light. Mistakes can be costly. There are also silver dollar coins.

Currency exchange. While banks and other financial offices will exchange currency, there is no need; major casino cages will do so immediately and without commission. This is the first and best choice for exchanging cash.

Credit cards. It's a good idea to carry at least one major credit card with you while in Las Vegas. With the advent of checking-based Visa cards, their acceptance in stores, restaurants, and bars is nearly universal. You will, however, still need some cash for tipping (see TIPPING), as well as for the slot machines.

Travelers' checks. Travelers' checks are accepted almost everywhere, though their relative complexity compared to credit cards makes them best for transporting cash between home and the casino cage, which will convert them into American currency as you require. You need to present your passport to exchange them for cash. **ATMs** are accessible throughout all major casinos. Beware of additional service fees – often up to $2; these will be listed on the ATM itself.

Taxes. Taxation in Nevada is generally low in comparison to other US cities, thanks to heavy taxes on gaming revenue. Sales tax on merchandise and restaurant food is 7.75 percent; food (groceries) purchased in stores is exempt from sales tax. Lodging taxes are 9 percent, except Downtown, where some taxes are 11 percent. In addition, many hotels assess 'resort fees' to offset rising energy costs.

O

OPENING HOURS

Las Vegas is a 24-hour town. The hotel-casinos and most of the city's bars never close. Though all casinos have at least one 24-hour coffee shop, most restaurants keep shorter hours, closing by 10pm, 11pm on Saturday and Sunday. Retail stores and malls, both on- and off-Strip, open between 9 and 10am, closing at about 9pm (although some 'destination shopping centers,' like the Forum Shops, open until midnight). Grocery and many drugstores are open 24 hours.

P

POLICE (see also CRIME AND SAFETY)

With 1.9 million residents and 37 million visitors annually, Las Vegas police take their work very seriously. They are generally helpful, and will guide tourists in the right direction if asked. Due to traffic problems, however, they are unusually strict about jay-walking, so pedestrians should take care to observe signs, lights, and directions. Casually uniformed bicycle patrols on the Strip and Downtown have helped improve the public face of the LVPD. Call **911** in an emergency.

POST OFFICES

Local post offices are open 8am–5pm weekdays and 9am–1pm on Saturdays. There is one at 3100 South Industrial Road; use the main post office at 301 Stewart Avenue if you need longer opening hours (6.30am–10pm Monday–Friday; 8am–4pm Saturday).

PUBLIC TRANSPORTATION

A **monorail** system runs along the east side of the Strip, from the MGM Grand to the Sahara. Single-ride tickets or day passes are available. A semi-private monorail connects certain casinos on the Strip's western side. Hopes are that the monorail will eventually extend all the way to Downtown, although no dates have been set. Plans also call for the monorail to continue south to the airport. The other main source of public transportation is the **Citizens Area Transit** buses, or CAT for short. Buses along the Strip, Downtown, and the Boulder Highway run 24 hours. On the Strip, CAT's red double-decker 'Deuce' buses run every 6–15 minutes, depending on the time of day. The 35 or so other citywide buses run 5.30am–1.30am, seven days a week.

T

TAXIS

Taxis are preferred by most tourists, but be warned: they are plentiful at all hotel *porte cacheres*, but nearly impossible to obtain by the streetside hailing method. You are better off walking up to a hotel and hiring one there. Further, calling a cab from a far-flung distance often requires up to an hour-long wait (see also TIPPING).

TELEPHONES

The country code for the US is 1; the area code for Clark County (where Las Vegas is located) is 702. While in the Vegas area, calls within the metropolitan vicinity need only the seven-digit number that follows the area code. International calls require 011 + country code + number. Be aware that hotels hike up the price of calls enormously.

TICKETS

Hotels have their own box offices, many of which accept over-the-phone purchases with a credit card. Tickets for some hotel events, as well as most other major events in Las Vegas (concerts, sporting events) can be purchased via **Ticketmaster** at 702-474 4000; there are Ticketmaster locations in Smith's supermarkets and several shopping malls. Remember, there are surcharges for using ticketing services, so prices will be cheaper if you buy direct from the venue's box office.

TIME DIFFERENCES

The US is divided into four time zones; Las Vegas is in the Pacific Time Zone, which is eight hours behind Greenwich Mean Time. Las Vegas operates on Daylight Saving Time; in mid-March, clocks move ahead by one hour, and then fall back by one hour in late October.

Las Vegas noon	New York 12pm	London 5pm	Jo'burg 7pm	Sydney 3am (next day)

TIPPING

Tipping (often called 'tokes' in Las Vegas) is the grease that keeps the machine of Las Vegas operating, far more than in other American cities. Most tourist service employees depend on tips as an important portion of their income. Tipping is simpler and less trouble if you carry a selection of dollars in the $1, $5, and $10 denominations with you for this purpose.

Most tipping is in the $2–$5 range, but sometimes a larger tip will help things move along. No table available at a big hotel restaurant for hours? A $10 or $20 bill will usually get you a seat immediately. Valet parking full? Try $5 first, more if it is a holiday or special event, and a space will often magically appear. If at valet pick-up a huge group of people are already waiting for their cars, waits of up to 20 minutes are not uncommon; however, a bill with the right picture on it handed to the ticket taker with a request to speed up the process will almost always have you out pretty quickly. When you tip under these circumstances, do so discreetly.

Restaurant tipping ranges between 15 to 20 percent of the total bill before taxes. A good tipper will go to 25 percent for extraordinary service. Be warned: some restaurants automatically include a 15 percent surcharge for large tables; you may argue the charge if service is poor. If it *is* included, you may of course add a small percentage for exceptional service. Remember, if service is bad, you are

not obligated to tip, but select another server the next time you visit
that establishment. Here are some general suggestions, but when in
doubt, always overtip: in Las Vegas, this may improve your vacation immeasurably:

Bartenders	$1–$2 per round for two or more
Bellmen	$1–$2 per bag
Cocktail Waitresses	$1–$2 per round
Concierges	$5 and up, depending on service
Doormen	$1 per bag, $1 for cab call
Limo Drivers	15 percent of total bill
Maids	$2 per day, left at the end of stay
Pool Attendants	$1
Taxi Drivers	20 percent
Valet Parking	$2 when car is returned; $5–$10 to find a spot on a busy night; $5 to ticket taker for fast return
Wait Staff (Restaurant)	15–20 percent of total before taxes
Wait Staff (Showroom)	$5–$10

Tipping in Casinos

Change Attendants	5 percent and up, depending on your luck and their interaction.
Cocktail Waitresses	$1, particularly if the drink is free; tipping with gaming chips is acceptable as well.
Dealers	If you are winning, tip the dealer by plac-ing a bet for him or her, one-half of your bet; when leaving the table in the black, tip according to your conscience.

TOURIST INFORMATION OFFICES

Contact the **Las Vegas Convention and Visitors Authority** for
tourist information at 3150 Paradise Road, Las Vegas, NV 89109,
tel: 702-892 0711, <www.visitlasvegas.com>.

W

WEBSITES AND ONLINE RESOURCES

Internet cafes can be hard to find in the US. The nearest equivalent is usually an office bureau like Kinko's, which offers internet access, but at a high cost. Wireless access is available in most hotels for an extra daily fee and at some coffee shops along the Strip and Downtown. Public libraries in Las Vegas offer internet access at no charge. The Las Vegas Library is at 833 Las Vegas Boulevard North, tel: 702-507 3600. There are also facilities in most hotel business centers, though these are expensive.

If you want to investigate Las Vegas on-line before you leave home, the following are some websites to help you do it:

www.visitlasvegas.com The official website of the Las Vegas Visitors and Convention Authority.

www.vegas.com Operated by the parent company of the *Las Vegas Sun*, *Las Vegas Life*, *Las Vegas Weekly* and countless others, this is perhaps the most comprehensive collection of information about the city on the net.

www.lasvegas.com Another fairly comprehensive site, especially for show tickets and finding out about upcoming events.

www.lasvegasadvisor.com Maintained by one of the city's best resource centers, it's particularly strong on gaming information.

www.lvol.com Las Vegas On line concentrates on entertainment and hotel information.

Y

YOUTH HOSTELS

There is only one hostel in town, the **Sin City Hostel** (1208 Las Vegas Boulevard South; tel: 702-868 0222) between the Strip and Downtown. The neighborhood is not the best, but safe during the day; be sure to travel in a crowd – or at least in pairs – at night.

Recommended Hotels

There are at least 130,000 hotel rooms in Las Vegas. This makes selecting accommodations intimidating, but not impossible. Consider the usual factors – cost, location, and budget – as well as how integral you want your hotel to be to your visit. It is possible, though not advisable, to visit Las Vegas and never leave your hotel premises.

The following is a recommended selection of Sin City's best hotels in four price categories. For a comprehensive listing of available hotels and motels, contact the Las Vegas Convention and Visitors Authority (see page 109).

All businesses must comply with the 'Americans with Disabilities' Act, and so are wheelchair accessible. Newer properties are the easiest to navigate, older and Downtown properties slightly more difficult.

All hotels accept all major credit cards (Visa, Mastercard, American Express), but price ranges listed do not include suites. Expect holiday and weekend rates to be significantly higher, and be sure to ask for specific quotes for your intended stay, a special package deal can cut costs considerably. For more information about most of these hotels, particularly with regard to their casinos and attractions, see pages 28–57.

$$$$	over $200
$$$	$100–$200
$$	$50–$100
$	under $50

STRIP CASINOS AND RESORTS

Bally's Hotel and Casino $$$ *3645 Las Vegas Boulevard South, tel: 702-739 4111, toll free: 1-800-634 3434, fax: 702-967 4405, <www.ballyslv.com>*. Bally's is one of the oldest hotels on the Strip, but also one of the most overlooked. Large rooms with a modern flair feature overstuffed furniture and subdued earthtones. The hotel has a beautiful pool area that is perfect for hot days. 2,814 rooms.

Bellagio Hotel and Casino $$$$ *3600 Las Vegas Boulevard South, tel:* 702-693 7111, *toll free:* 1-888-987 6667, *fax:* 702-792 7646, *<www.bellagioresort.com>*. One of the city's most lavish resorts, Bellagio proves the type of Italian replication $1.6 billion can buy. The standard guest rooms are satisfyingly plush, decorated in shades of brown, black, and cream. Two key perks are the comfortable beds and huge bathrooms with deep-soaking tubs and showers big enough for two. Tip: be sure to ask for a room overlooking the fountains, as there is in-room music on the TV dial that is choreographed to the water show. Theme: Italian/Mediterranean elegance. 4,445 rooms.

Bill's Las Vegas $$ *3595 Las Vegas Boulevard South, tel:* 702-737 2100, *toll free:* 1-866-245 5745, *<www.billslasvegas.com>*. Wedged in a corner of Las Vegas Boulevard between Bally's and the Flamingo, the rooms here offer a charming and comfortable rendition of the 'City by the Bay' *circa* 1900, featuring brass beds and etched mirrors. A big draw of the hotel-casino is the recently added restaurant, Drai's. Theme: Old San Francisco. 200 rooms.

Caesars Palace Hotel and Casino $$$ *3570 Las Vegas Boulevard South, tel:* 702-731 7110, *toll free:* 1-800-634 6661, *fax:* 702-731 7172, *<www.caesars.com>*. A standard-setter since its opening, elegance at Caesars seems within reach of anyone. A recent renovation – including a new tower and pool – raises the level of its already excellent accommodations, where marble and mahogany abound. Baths feature oversize marble tubs and European fixtures, and rooms are tastefully decorated with art and sculpture. Theme: ancient Rome. 3,348 rooms.

Circus Circus Hotel and Casino $$ *2880 Las Vegas Boulevard South, tel:* 702-734 0410, *toll free:* 1-800-444 2472, *fax:* 702-734 5897, *<www.circuscircus.com>*. Circus Circus is Las Vegas's original family-friendly, low-roller hotel-casino. Rooms are typical chain hotel style, with blue carpeting and blonde wood furniture. To stay in the newer rooms, request one in the West Tower. Circus Circus will be partly demolished and the remainder refurbished and greatly expanded in the near future as part of a large multiple-use project. Theme: the Big Top, though not in the rooms. 3,774 rooms.

Excalibur Hotel and Casino $$ *3850 Las Vegas Boulevard South, tel: 702-597 7777, toll free: 1-800-937 7777, fax: 702-597 7009, <www.excaliburcasino.com>.* Excalibur offers a Renaissance Faire experience aimed squarely at families and travelers on a budget. Rooms are surprisingly restrained considering the hotel's gaudy exterior, with wrought-iron accents over dark wood and contemporary touches of red, blue, and green. Theme: Medieval Fantasy. 4,008 rooms.

Flamingo Las Vegas $$$ *3555 Las Vegas Boulevard South, tel: 702-733 3111, toll free: 1-800-732 2111, fax: 702-733 3353, <www.flamingolv.com>.* The Flamingo retains its vintage desert oasis flavor with a large, lush tropical pool and garden area, complete with a wildlife habitat. One of the oldest resorts on the Strip (1946), the Flamingo still manages to hold its own in the middle of all the upstarts. Theme: the Tropics. 3,642 rooms.

Four Seasons Hotel Las Vegas $$$$ *3960 Las Vegas Boulevard South, tel: 702-632 5000, toll free: 1-877-632 5000, <www.fourseasons.com/lasvegas>.* The Four Seasons offers quiet, ultra-luxurious accommodations on the upper floors of the Mandalay Bay tower, accessed only via a private lobby elevator. The two-story main building houses the lobby, four restaurants and bars, a health spa, and meeting rooms. A large pool set in a lush garden is available only to Four Seasons guests. 424 rooms.

Harrah's Las Vegas $$$ *3475 Las Vegas Boulevard South, tel: 702-369 5000, toll free: 1-800-427 7247, fax: 702-369 5008, <www.harrahslasvegas.com>.* Bright colors, light wood, and brass fixtures lend an upbeat feel to the accommodations in this venerable resort, which itself has a light, outdoorsy atmosphere. Jacuzzi tubs are available. Theme: Carnival. 2,579 rooms.

Imperial Palace Hotel and Casino $$ *3535 Las Vegas Boulevard South, tel: 702-731 3311, toll free: 1-800-634 6441, fax: 702-735*

8578, <www.imperialpalace.com>. This sprawling complex houses quite a few average but comfortable rooms. The adventurous can rent a suite with a mirrored Jacuzzi tub and mirrored ceiling over the bed, while the pool area with tumbling waterfall is large and tranquil. Theme: Oriental Palace. 2,700 rooms.

Luxor Hotel and Casino $$–$$$ *3900 Las Vegas Boulevard South, tel: 702-262 4444, toll free: 1-888-777 0188, <www.luxor.com>.* The Luxor consists of a 30-story Egyptian pyramid and two towers. The rooms in the pyramid have one sloping glass wall overlooking the main floor, and most have a shower but no tub (rooms in the towers do have tubs). The rooms feature art deco and Egyptian-inspired furnishings with marble bathrooms, but the resort is in the process of updating its image. Many family-friendly attractions are here, and discount rates are often available. 4,400 rooms.

Mandalay Bay Resort and Casino $$$ *3950 Las Vegas Boulevard South, tel: 702-632 7777 or 877-632 7800, <www.mandalaybay. com>.* Guests at the Mandalay will enjoy an 11-acre (4-hectare) tropical environment, including a wave pool, an enormous spa, and a number of trendy restaurants, including the House of Blues. The decor is lovely and low-key, with a terrific range of warm-weather souvenirs (parasols, fans, sandals) in the giftshop. Theme: luxurious urban tropical jungle. 3,700 rooms, including a new tower and a convention center.

MGM Grand Hotel and Casino $$$ *3799 Las Vegas Boulevard South, tel: 702-891 7777, toll free: 1-800-929 1111, fax: 702-891 1030, <www.mgmgrand.com>.* Four distinct towers result in four different types of room themes. The nicest are in the Hollywood tower, with gold-speckled walls surrounding maple and cherry furniture. Gilded accents and framed photos of classic film stars add up to the classy experience. The other towers – Casablanca, Old South, and Oz – feature rooms that also relate to their names. Theme: City of Entertainment. 5,034 rooms.

Mirage Hotel and Casino $$$ *3400 Las Vegas Boulevard South, tel: 702-791 7111, toll free: 1-800-374-9000, fax: 702-791 7446,*

<www.mirage.com>. A lovely Polynesian resort, despite being the oldest of the city's post-1950s additions. The rooms have a distinctive beach resort feel, with subdued neutral colors and gold accents. Most have marbled entries and baths, as well as canopied beds. Though the rooms are somewhat small, they are very pleasant. Theme: South Seas. 3,000 rooms.

Monte Carlo Hotel and Casino $$$ *3770 Las Vegas Boulevard South, tel: 702-730 7777, toll free: 1-800-311 8999, fax: 702-730 7250, <www.monte-carlo.com>*. Striking in its understated European theme, this resort captures an air of popular beauty. The outdoor area is particularly lush. Rooms are classically European in flavor and very comfortable. Theme: old-European elegance. 3,014 rooms.

New York-New York Hotel and Casino $$$ *3790 Las Vegas Boulevard South, tel: 702-740 6969, toll free: 1-800-815 4365, fax: 702-740 6920, <www.nynyhotelcasino.com>*. Taking theming to its extreme, rooms here are done in 62 unique styles, all related to the 'Big Apple.' Art deco is the overall inspiration, with round-top furnishings and inlaid wood galore. On average, the rooms (and their bathrooms) are small, but the overall experience is pleasant. Theme: New York City. 2,034 rooms.

Paris Hotel and Casino $$$ *3655 Las Vegas Boulevard South, tel: 702-946 7000, toll free: 1-888-266 5687, fax: 702-946 4405, <www.parislasvegas.com>*. Paris Las Vegas is modeled after the City of Light's Hôtel de Ville, with numerous replicas of Parisian landmarks, including the Eiffel Tower, Rue de la Paix, the Paris Opera House, the Louvre, and the Arc de Triomphe. Food – as you would expect – is excellent. Theme: classic France. 2,916 rooms.

Planet Hollywood $$$ *3667 Las Vegas Boulevard South, tel: 702-785 5555, toll free: 1-866-919 7472, <www.planethollywoodresort. com>*. Built on the site of the old Aladdin, this hotel was completely renovated inside and out in 2006–7, trading its former Middle Eastern look for a hip, young ambience of glass, polished steel and black tile. Theme: Sunset Strip. 2,567 rooms.

Riviera Hotel and Casino $$ *2901 Las Vegas Boulevard South, tel: 702-734 5110, toll free: 1-800-634 6753, fax: 702-794 9451, <www.rivierahotel.com>.* One of the older Strip resorts, the Monaco and Monte Carlo towers house the newest, nicest rooms, each richly decorated with mahogany furniture and burgundy fabrics. Most tower rooms offer views of the pool or mountains; the scenery from the original nine-story structure is less rewarding. 2,286 rooms.

Sahara Hotel and Casino $$ *2535 Las Vegas Boulevard South, tel: 702-737 2111, toll free: 1-888-696 2121, fax: 702-791 2027, <www.saharavegas.com>.* A recent $100-million renovation went the usual Vegas route, replacing a dark and plush atmosphere with lighter decor. The result is one of attractive comfort for tour groups, conventioneers, and mid-budget travelers. Rooms are bright, utilizing lots of earth-tones and wood. Theme: Moroccan Palace. 1,758 rooms.

Stratosphere Hotel and Casino $$ *2000 Las Vegas Boulevard South, tel: 702-380 7777, toll free: 1-800-998 6937, fax: 702-383 5334, <www.stratlv.com>.* Unfortunately, there are no rooms in the big tower. Instead, accommodations are located in one of the mid-rise towers. Rooms are surprisingly comfortable, nicely decorated with art deco touches and black lacquer. The semi-central location, however – not quite the Strip, not quite Downtown – leaves the Stratosphere out on its own. 2,444 rooms.

T.I. (Treasure Island) $$$ *3300 Las Vegas Boulevard South, tel: 702-894 7111, toll free: 1-800-944 7444, fax: 702-894 7414, <www.treasureisland.com>.* A recent renovation has ditched the kid-oriented motif in favor of a more grown-up theme. Affordable and comfortable – though not elaborate – rooms are housed in a Y-shaped tower. Rooms on the Strip face the pirate battle outside, though the view might be obscured. Other accommodations look out over the Mirage casino or the mountains. Theme: sexy Sirens of the sea take on renegade pirates. 2,900 rooms.

Tropicana Resort and Casino $$$ *3801 Las Vegas Boulevard South, tel: 702-739 2222, toll free: 1-800-634 4000, fax: 702-739*

2469, *<www.tropicanalv.com>*. Aimed at adult travelers, the hotel is a slice of subtly themed Polynesia – bamboo and wood dominate. Guest rooms in the Island tower have a tropical theme, while the Paradise tower's rooms lean toward French Provincial. The tropical pool area (with swim-up blackjack tables) is lush and relaxing. Theme: low-key Hawaiian. 2,000 rooms.

The Venetian Resort Hotel-Casino $$$ *3355 Las Vegas Boulevard South, tel: 702-414 1000, toll free: 1-888-283 6423, fax: 702-414 1100, <www.venetian.com>*. Renaissance Italy is captured in dramatic architecture and landscaping, including canals with operating gondolas. A four-level entertainment plaza has a showroom, and the Grand Canal Shoppes contain 140 stores and restaurants. Theme: traditional Venice. 4,049 rooms, including a new tower.

Wynn Las Vegas $$$$ *3131 Las Vegas Boulevard South, tel: 702-770 7100, toll free: 1-888-320 WYNN, fax: 702-770 1571, <www.wynnlasvegas.com>*. Las Vegas's newest resort also claims to be its most lavish. From the 'mountain' at its entrance to the lagoons and waterfalls at the back, no expense has been spared to create a luxurious hideaway on the Strip for anyone with enough money to pay for paradise. Theme: Mother Nature for millionaires. 2,700 rooms.

DOWNTOWN CASINOS AND RESORTS

Binion's Gambling Hall and Hotel $$ *128 Fremont Street, tel: 702-382 1600, toll free: 1-800 237 6537, fax: 702-382 5750, <www.binions.com>*. Binion's may be the most traditional gambling joint left in town. The 'Place that Made Poker Famous' has some of the highest betting limits in the world, and the comfortable accommodations are modestly priced. 366 rooms.

California Hotel and Casino $$ *12 Ogden Avenue, tel: 702-385 1222, toll free: 1-800-634 6505, fax: 702-388 2610, <www.thecal.com>*. This hotel draws guests mostly from Hawaii and Asia, though all visitors are welcome. The California's decor offers a taste of the

South Seas rather than the Wild West; the rooms, however, are more contemporary in style, complete with marble baths. Located off Fremont Street. 856 rooms.

El Cortez Hotel and Casino $ *600 Fremont Street, tel: 702-385 5200, toll free: 1-800-634 6703, fax: 702-385 1554, <www.elcortez hotelcasino.com>.* El Cortez, the city's oldest operating casino (built in 1941), underwent a $12 million restoration in 2007 to become a centerpiece of the Fremont East Entertainment District. The most pleasant rooms are in the 14-story tower, but the older rooms are still fine. Clean and comfortable, but not extravagant. 400 rooms.

Fitzgerald's Casino Hotel $$ *301 Fremont Street, tel: 702-388 2400, toll free: 1-800-274 5825, fax: 702-388 2478, <www.fitz geralds.com>.* Many rooms offer nice views of the city and mountains within comfortable surroundings. Accommodations are of the standard Holiday Inn variety, and within a mid-budget price range. Attractive views of the Fremont Street Experience can also be enjoyed in this (mostly) low-roller haven. 638 rooms.

4 Queens Hotel and Casino $$ *202 Fremont Street, tel: 702-385 4011, toll free: 1-800-634 6045, fax: 702-387 5185, <www.four queens.com>.* A neon landmark since 1966, the 4 Queens today entices mainly older guests. Rooms are of Southwestern or earth-tone decor and are pleasant and affordable. Four restaurants include Hugo's Cellar, an always-busy classic Las Vegas gourmet room with an award-winning wine list. 690 rooms.

Fremont Hotel and Casino $$ *200 East Fremont Street, tel: 702-385 3232, toll free: 1-800-634 6460, fax: 702-385 6229, <www. fremontcasino.com>.* Constructed in 1956 as Las Vegas's first highrise building, the Fremont's guest rooms are comfortable, modern, and decorated in a tropical-floral style. The hotel hosts many Hawaiian travelers and so the Second Street Grill features Pacific Rim specialties. 447 rooms and suites.

Golden Gate Hotel and Casino $ *1 Fremont Street, tel: 702-385 1906, toll free: 1-800-426 1906, fax: 702-383 9681, <www.golden*

gatecasino.net>. This charmingly old-fashioned operation is the city's oldest hotel. Its small (120 sq ft/12 sq m) rooms, with plaster walls and mahogany doors, hark back to another era. Rates are low, and the location at the west end of the Fremont Street Experience couldn't be better. 100 rooms.

Golden Nugget $$$ *129 East Fremont Street, tel: 702-385 7111, toll free: 1-800-846 5336, fax: 702-386 8362, <www.goldennugget. com>.* The 1946 Golden Nugget is the jewel of Downtown; metropolitan elegance supersedes the surrounding glitz. Guests, greeted by uniformed doormen, enter a gilded lobby full of marble and crystal. Accommodations – featuring a misted pool area landscaped with palms – are luxurious enough to have earned a top AAA rating. 1,907 rooms.

Main Street Station $$ *200 North Main Street, tel: 702-387 1896, toll free: 1-800-713 8933, fax: 702-386 4466, <www.main streetcasino.com>.* Main Street Station is Las Vegas's best-kept secret, as the Victorian-styled casino is filled with expensive antiques. Rooms are spacious, quiet, and simply decorated, with shutters instead of drapes. Dining options include several very good restaurants. 406 rooms.

Plaza Hotel and Casino $ *1 Main Street, tel: 702-386 2110, toll free: 1-800-634 6575, fax: 702-382 8281, <http://plazahotel casino.com>.* A few steps from the Greyhound bus station and seen in almost all photographs of neon-lit Downtown, this high-rise hotel has its own wedding chapel as well as exercise facilities, a swimming pool, three restaurants, a concierge desk, cable TV, and even its own shuttle to the airport. Great value for the price. 1,000 rooms.

OFF-STRIP CASINOS AND RESORTS

Alexis Park $$$ *375 East Harmon, tel: 702-796 3330, toll free: 1-800-582 2228, fax: 702-796 4334, <www.alexispark.com>.* A Mediterranean villa on 20 acres (8 hectares) of beautifully landscaped grounds, this resort offers volumes beyond the typical Las

Vegas hotel. Styled with classy European elegance, all rooms are suites, with 10 distinct floor plans and different decor throughout. A lack of gaming means the place is noticeably quiet, but the Alexis is directly across from the Hard Rock Hotel and Casino if you're in the mood to hit the tables. 500 rooms.

Boulder Station Hotel and Casino $$ *4111 Boulder Highway, 89121, tel: 702-432 7777, toll free: 1-800-683 7777, fax: 702-432 7744, <www.boulderstation.com>.* Located on the Boulder Strip going out of town, the Boulder Station Hotel offers a small-scale version of the inclusive upscale resort. Rooms are comfortable and attractive, but a bit higher-priced than other low-key off-Strip resorts. 300 rooms.

Gold Coast Hotel and Casino $$ *4000 West Flamingo Road, tel: 702-367-7111, toll free: 1-800-331 5334, fax: 702-385 7505, <www.goldcoastcasino.com>.* The Gold Coast Hotel, located one mile (1.5km) west of the strip, offers a combination of entertainment and gaming, as well as a bowling center, three lounges, a dance hall, and a theater. Guest rooms are both comfortable and affordable. 711 rooms.

Hard Rock Hotel and Casino $$$ *4455 Paradise Road, tel: 702-693 5000, toll free: 1-800-693 7625, fax: 702-693 5010, <www.hardrockhotel.com>.* A surprising exercise in casual elegance, the Hard Rock's rooms are spacious and pleasing, decorated in a classic Modernist style. Light fixtures made of cymbals adorn the ceilings. All bedrooms have balconies, though the ones with a pool views are preferable. Theme: rock and roll. 700 rooms.

Las Vegas Hilton Hotel and Casino $$$ *3000 South Paradise Road, tel: 702-732 5111, toll free: 1-888-732 7117, fax: 702-794 3611, <www.lvhilton.com>.* Located next to the Convention Center, the Hilton does brisk business during large conventions. The lobby and casino are gracious and expensively outfitted, and the already plush guest rooms – each loaded with overstuffed chairs, large closets, and marble-tiled bathrooms – recently underwent a complete renovation. 3,174 rooms.

Orleans Hotel and Casino $$ *4500 West Tropicana Avenue, tel: 702-365 7111, toll free: 1-800-675 3267, fax: 702-365 7505, <www.orleanscasino.com>.* The guest rooms here are among the city's largest, and are often an excellent bargain. They are lavishly appointed, with decor in brass, antiques, and lace. Theme: the Big Easy. 1,185 rooms.

Palace Station Hotel and Casino $$ *2411 West Sahara Avenue, tel: 702-367 2411, toll free: 1-800-634 3101, fax: 702-367 2478, <www.palacestation.com>.* Located just off the Strip near Interstate 15, the Palace Station's best rooms are within the tower, built in 1991, while original rooms are in a two-story building surrounding the pool. If possible, request one of the corner rooms, which have larger bathrooms. 1,030 rooms.

Palms Casino Resort $$$ *4321 West Flamingo Road, tel: 702-942 7777, toll free: 1-866-942 7777, fax: 702-942 7001, <www.palms. com>.* A favorite haunt of celebrities, the Palms offers luxury rooms and suites and boasts its own recording studio and one of Las Vegas's top concert venues, as well as popular nightclubs that include ghostbar and the world's only Playboy Club. 439 rooms.

Red Rock Casino Resort and Spa $$$ *11011 West Charleston, tel: 702-797 7777, toll free: 1-666-767 7773, <www.redrocklasvegas. com>.* Far from the Strip but convenient for Red Rock Canyon and Mount Charleston, this new, ultra-elegant spa resort features bike, horseback and kayak 'adventure-spa' packages. 814 rooms.

Rio All-Suite Hotel and Casino $$$ *3700 West Flamingo Road, tel: 702-252 7777, toll free: 1-866-746 7671, fax: 702-252 8909, <www.riolasvegas.com>.* The Rio offers such quality that it has received international acclaim (it's one of the city's best values). The newer accommodations are in the Masquerade Tower, but even standard rooms are still well on the large side. Decor is a contemporary style of bold colors and wood. 2,556 rooms.

Sam's Town Hotel and Casino $$ *5111 Boulder Highway, 89122, tel: 702-456 7777, toll free: 1-800-897 8696, fax: 702-454 8017,*

<www.samstown.com>. The rustic Wild West and Native American decor may sound kitschy, but the rooms here are actually quiet, comfortable, and attractive. The real treat is the nine-story atrium over an indoor park, complete with live trees, running water, and footpaths. Some in-facing rooms below the ninth floor are within this atrium. 650 rooms.

Sunset Station $$ *1301 West Sunset Road, 89119, tel: 702-547 7777, toll free: 1-888-786 7389, fax: 702-547 7744, <www.sunset station.com>*. The Mediterranean interior of the Sunset Station is really quite stunning. Amenities include a 13-screen movie theater and KidsQuest indoor play area, making this a sure-fire family winner. Sunset Station is located far off the Strip in Green Valley, across from a major shopping area. 450 rooms.

MOTELS

Crest Budget Motel $ *207 North Sixth Street, tel: 702-382 5642, fax: 702-382 8038*. Downtown motel with cable TV, microwave ovens and complementary coffee and breakfast.

Days Inn Downtown $ *707 East Fremont Street, tel: 702-388 1400, toll free: 1-800-325 2344, fax: 702-388 9622*. This chain motel has an elevated pool, a sundeck, a restaurant, and even its own slot-machine parlor.

Howard Johnson $–$$ *1401 Las Vegas Boulevard, tel: 702-388 0301, toll free: 1-800-325 2344, fax: 702-388 2506, <www.hojo. com>*. Located near the Convention Center, this motel has an Olympic-size pool, a restaurant, and a wedding chapel.

King Albert Motel $ *185 Albert Avenue, tel: 702-732 1555, toll free: 1-800-553 7753*. This budget-priced motel off the Strip has a swimming pool, a laundromat, and kitchenettes.

Motel 6 $ *195 East Tropicana Avenue, tel: 702-798 0728*. Three blocks from the Strip and not far from the airport, this motel has a swimming pool, a food store, and plenty of parking.

Recommended Restaurants

Restaurants here are listed alphabetically and according to location. Price ranges are per person for a typical main course. A large tip of 15–20 percent is appropriate, and often expected; this should be left on the table after the meal.

Outstanding buffets are listed in this section, with the name of the hotel first. Expect to stand in line (and pay) for a buffet before you enter. Once inside, you can eat all you wish, though it is considered unacceptable to bring food out of the buffet area. Soft drinks are often included in the price of the buffet, but beer and wine is purchased separately at the register. For more information about the dining scene in Las Vegas, see Eating Out on page 104.

All of the restaurants listed below accept major credit cards (Visa, Mastercard, and American Express)

$$$$	$30 and over
$$$	$25–$30
$$	$13–$24
$	under $12

STRIP RESTAURANTS

Bertolini's $$ *Caesars Palace Forum Shops*, tel: 702-735 4663. Lunch and dinner. This upscale franchise offers delicious Italian entrees and wood-fired pizza. Most patrons choose to dine 'outdoors' near a huge (and loud) fountain.

Canaletto $–$$$$ *Venetian Grand Canal Shoppes*, tel: 702-733 0070. Lunch and dinner. Although the food at Canaletto is pleasant, the experience of dining by the waterside while sitting in the middle of a desert is the one to write home about.

Cheesecake Factory $$ *Caesars Palace Forum Shops*, tel: 702-792 6888. Breakfast, lunch, and dinner. The Factory is a cavernous restaurant with a huge menu offering a variety of food. Sunday brunch (not buffet) is delicious. Though you might be tempted to sit mall-side, don't do it – the statue water show is pretty noisy and can be disruptive.

Chinois $$$ *Caesars Palace Forum Shops, tel: 702-737 9700*. Lunch and dinner. A Wolfgang Puck creation, this is an upscale Pan-Asian affair where diners enjoy selections from an innovative menu. The cafe section is less expensive than the dining room.

Diego's $$$ *MGM Grand, tel: 702-891 3200*. Dinner only. Decorated in bright reds and pinks, this contemporary Mexican restaurant serves traditional fare, such as *pollo en mole* and *cochinita pibil*, and offers Las Vegas's largest selection of tequilas.

Drai's $$$ *Bill's Las Vegas, tel: 702-737 0555*. Dinner only. Restaurateur to the stars in Hollywood, Victor Drai's eatery has made the Barbary Coast Hotel a great place to eat. The menu is elaborate French nouvelle, and the appetizers are delicious.

Emeril's $$$ *MGM Grand, tel: 702-891 7374*. Lunch and dinner. Seafood was almost unheard of in the desert until Emeril Lagasse arrived. Imaginative preparations result in amazingly delicate dining experiences, with a great wine list to top it all off.

Mirage Buffet $ *The Mirage, tel: 702-891 7374*. Breakfast, lunch, and dinner. An excellent, all-you-can-eat feast. Though a little expensive, the overall quality, fabulous salad selection, and delicious desserts make this a winner.

Mon Ami Gabi $–$$$ *Paris Las Vegas, tel: 702-944 GABI*. Lunch and dinner. Enjoy the passing crowds from this raised café backed by a facade of the Louvre, and the lake show across the street. Order classic steak-frites or the fruites de mer; seafood is flown in daily.

Noodles $$ *Bellagio, tel: 702-693 8131*. Lunch and dinner. A modern Tony Chi-designed Pan-Asian noodle shop in the heart of Las Vegas. The Modernist touches are elegantly trendy, and the variety of menu selections vast and authentic.

Palm $$$$ *Caesars Palace Forum Shops, tel: 702-732 7256*. Lunch and dinner. A steakhouse of near perfection that also serves lobster. The wine list is extensive, with many by-the-glass choices.

Picasso $$$$ *Bellagio, tel: 702-693 7223*. Dinner only. The French cooking of master chef Julian Serrano has ensured that Picasso is now a restaurant of not just local, but national importance. While you're waiting for the next culinary treat, admire the art on the walls. They really are by that other, even more famous, master.

Rainforest Café $$ *MGM Grand, tel: 702-891 8580*. Breakfast, lunch, and dinner. Kids love this loud, family-style restaurant with its lush jungle environment, life-size animatronic beasts, and simulated thunderstorms. The entrance is through an arched aquarium. The menu offers standard American fare under exotic names.

Spago $$$ *Caesars Palace Forum Shops, tel: 702-369 6300*. Lunch and dinner. One of the first Los Angeles eateries to introduce fusion cooking techniques, Wolfgang Puck's Las Vegas restaurant is as much about being seen there as it is eating there. A French-, Asian-, and Italian-inspired menu ends with fabulous desserts.

Top of the World $$$$ *Stratosphere Tower, tel: 702-380 7711*. Lunch and dinner. The food often takes second place here, as the revolving restaurant offers a full-circle view of Vegas every hour. Though the view is unparalleled, the continental cuisine is not bad.

DOWNTOWN RESTAURANTS

Bay City Diner $ *Golden Gate Hotel, tel: 702-382 3510*. Open 24 hours a day. The Bay City Diner is an all-night café with a twist. A dark wood interior and turn-of-the-20th century feel lend a pleasant ambience to accompany an all-American comfort food menu.

Binion's Ranch Steakhouse $$$ *Binion's, tel: 702-382 1600*. Dinner only. Some of the best beef in the West comes through this steakhouse (the long-time owners, the Binions, were ranchers as well as casino-owners). Great 24th-floor view of the city.

The Buffet $ *Golden Nugget Hotel, tel: 702-385 7111.* Breakfast, lunch, and dinner. This is the buffet that set the modern standard. An elegant and comfortable dining room accommodates diners who choose from a variety of well-executed, all-you-can-eat fare.

Garden Court Buffet $ *Main Street Station, tel: 702-387 1896.* A relaxing buffet experience set under high ceilings, surrounded by marble and brick. Multiple food stations allow diners to sample everything from wood-fired pizzas to Mexican and Asian.

Hugo's Cellar $$$ *4 Queens, tel: 702-385 4011.* Dinner only. An excellent wine list complements this unexpected Downtown gem. The continental cuisine is a bit dated, but the experience is elegant and romantic.

Triple 7 Brewpub $ *Main Street Station, tel: 702-387 1896.* Open 11am–7am. The Triple 7 Brewpub is a virtually unknown (in Las Vegas) delight. Ales and beers brewed on the premises complement a fresh and innovative menu of American and Asian cuisine, as well as delicious wood-fired pizzas.

OFF-STRIP RESTAURANTS

Benihana Village $$$ *Las Vegas Hilton, tel: 702-732 5755.* Dinner only. The same Benihana experience you may have had in other US cities: an Asian eatery set in an elaborate garden. Energetic chefs entertain by cooking Japanese food in front of the diners.

Carnival World Buffet $ *Rio All-Suite Hotel and Casino, tel: 702-777 7777.* Breakfast, lunch, and dinner. The main attractions here are the numerous cooked-to-order food stations ranging from Asian to Mexican to Italian. The buffet combines a fresh-food approach with the mass-audience aesthetic.

Chicago Joe's $–$$ *820 South 4th Street, tel: 702-382 5637.* Lunch and dinner. Closed Mondays. A tiny restaurant in a former Downtown home, Joe's has been serving tasty southern Italian pastas and shellfish for over 30 years.

Dona Maria Tamales Restaurant $ *910 Las Vegas Boulevard South, tel: 702-382 6538.* Lunch and dinner. Dona Maria's is an authentic Mexican restaurant, specializing in tamales. The choice is a wide one: choose from hot pork, mild chicken, or chili-and-cheese varieties.

The Feast Buffet $ *Palace Station, tel: 702-367 2411.* The innovator of a modern buffet trend, the Feast was responsible for the live-action cooking now found in buffets citywide. Made-to-order omelets, multiple ethnic food stations, and a smorgasbord of desserts make this one of the best buffet bargains in town.

Gaylord India Restaurant $$ *Rio All-Suite Hotel, tel: 702-777 7923.* Dinner daily, brunch buffet Friday to Sunday. This spinoff location of San Francisco's famous Indian restaurant serves such specialties as tandoori prawns and lamb curry in a romantic atmosphere that showcases authentic Indian antiques.

Golden Steer Steakhouse $$$ *308 West Sahara Avenue, tel: 702-384 4470.* The Golden Steer is one of the classic Vegas steakhouses, with an atmosphere of a bordello. If you like big steaks served in dark booths, you'll love this place.

Hamada of Japan $$ *365 East Flamingo Road, tel: 702-733 3005.* Dinner, open until 4am. A lounge, sushi bar, and dining room combine to make this a major Japanese food experience. A favorite meal-time diversion is to watch your own food being cooked at the *hibachi* tables.

Hofbräuhaus $$ *4510 Paradise Road, tel: 702-853 2337, <www.hofbrauhauslasvegas.com>.* Lunch and dinner. A replica of Munich's famous four-century-old brewery, this huge restaurant across the street from the Hard Rock Hotel serves traditional Bavarian cuisine in a cheery Oktoberfest atmosphere.

Jazzed Café and Vinoteca $ *2055 East Tropicana Avenue, tel: 702-798 5995.* Dinner and late-night dining. This tiny, elegant, candle-lit cafe serves carefully crafted Tuscan specialties – risotto, pastas, and salads – complemented by an extensive wine list. Best of all, it is open until about 4am.

Lindo Michoacan $$ *2655 East Desert Inn Road, tel: 702-735 6828.* Lunch and dinner. This authentic Mexican restaurant serves elaborate south-of-the-border cuisine. Specialties include wonderful roasted goat meat that is served with rich sauces and freshly-made flour tortillas.

Mr Lucky's 24/7 $ *Hard Rock Hotel, tel: 702-693 5000.* Mr Lucky's is an 'always open' hotel restaurant that breaks the mold. In other words, it's not shabby and down-at-the-heels, but instead is nicely decorated and has a welcomingly festive atmosphere. The menu offers standard American classics such as hamburgers, steak, pizza, and pasta.

Paymon's Mediterranean Café $$ *4147 South Maryland Parkway, tel: 702-731 6030.* Lunch and dinner. With its tantalizing menu of Greek, Middle Eastern and Persian food, this deli-style eatery has been an award-winning local favorite for 20 years. It's one of the best places in town for vegetarian fare.

Ruth's Chris Steak House $$$ *3900 Paradise Road, tel: 702-791 7011.* Lunch and dinner daily. Ruth Fertel opened her first restaurant in New Orleans in 1965; now her exceedingly tasty steaks can be ordered all over the United States. There's another Ruth's Chris at *4561 West Flamingo Avenue* (dinner only).

Voo Doo Steak and Lounge $$ *Rio All-Suite Hotel and Casino, tel: 702-777 7923.* Dinner only. High atop the Rio, with a view overlooking all of Las Vegas, enjoy spicy Creole and Cajun specialties, served in a somewhat-decadent atmosphere.

Z'Tejas $$ *9560 West Sahara, tel: 702-638 0610.* Lunch and dinner. Z'Tejas has elevated Southwestern cooking to an art form. Appreciative diners enjoy jalapeno chicken pasta, vegetable enchiladas, and other spicy selections that are served in a modern, casually elegant atmosphere.

The
FLiP
FLOP
Club

Midnight Messages

Other books in
The Flip-Flop Club series:

Charmed Summer
Whale Song

Coming soon . . .

Star Struck

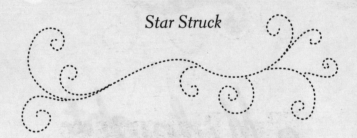

Midnight Messages

Ellen Richardson

Series created by Working Partners Ltd

OXFORD
UNIVERSITY PRESS

OXFORD
UNIVERSITY PRESS

Great Clarendon Street, Oxford OX2 6DP

Oxford University Press is a department of the University of Oxford.
It furthers the University's objective of excellence in research, scholarship,
and education by publishing worldwide in

Oxford   New York

Auckland   Cape Town   Dar es Salaam   Hong Kong   Karachi
Kuala Lumpur   Madrid   Melbourne   Mexico City   Nairobi
New Delhi   Shanghai   Taipei   Toronto

With offices in

Argentina   Austria   Brazil   Chile   Czech Republic   France   Greece
Guatemala   Hungary   Italy   Japan   Poland   Portugal   Singapore
South Korea   Switzerland   Thailand   Turkey   Ukraine   Vietnam

Oxford is a registered trade mark of Oxford University Press
in the UK and in certain other countries

British Library Cataloguing in Publication Data
Data available

ISBN: 978-0-19-275663-3
1 3 5 7 9 10 8 6 4 2

Printed in Great Britain

Paper used in the production of this book is a natural,
recyclable product made from wood grown in sustainable forests.
The manufacturing process conforms to the environmental
regulations of the country of origin.

Special dedication to Mollie from Renee, winner of the 'I Have the Best Friend Ever!' competition.

Mollie is the BEST FRIEND EVER because she is loyal to me, she respects me, she thinks of me often, and is there for me whenever I need her. We have lots of fun and laughs together! I don't think there would be a better friend than Mollie!!! Thank you Mollie for being such an AWESOME friend to me! BFFs :D

SUNDAY ISLAND

DEAD MAN'S

N
W E
S

THE HOOK

ROCKY
CLIFFS

Treeh

MIRROR
COVE

WESTERN
ISLES

MOUNTAIN
STREAM

LAKE

DEVIL'S
TEETH

Caravan Park

MAIN
BEACH

HARBOUR

Sailing
Club

EASTERN ISLES
SOMMER -ON- SEA
Stables
Sunday House
RING ROAD
CAUSEWAY
Village
Aunt Dina's Cottage

Chapter 1

Elly charged up the hill, her backpack bouncing with each step. The sun was setting and she was late for the sleepover at Tash's tree house.

It was Celeste's fault. Aunt Dina's friend was staying with them, and she was a little weird. She was obsessed with ghosts. Over supper Aunt Dina had mentioned that Sunday House was supposed to be haunted by the ghost of Tash's grandad, Old Man Blake. Celeste had spent the rest of the meal questioning Elly, even cornering her in the hall as she tried to leave. It had taken forever to escape.

The Blake family graveyard was just ahead. Elly could see the dark rectangle that was Old Man Blake's grave, which he had ordered be left open and unfilled. Elly skirted past the graveyard and gasped.

A shape loomed out of the gathering dusk. It stumbled towards her, tall, with misshapen shoulders and no head. Elly's heart lurched. It *couldn't* be human—but it had legs. And feet. And…flip-flops. Neon-pink ones. Another creature appeared, wearing sparkly purple flip-flops. Beside it trotted a small dog.

'Tash! Sierra!'

The border terrier, Mojo, darted up to Elly, barking in delight. Tash and Sierra peered around the cardboard boxes they were carrying.

'Oof!' Sierra dumped her boxes on the ground. 'Hey, you skiver!' She turned to Elly with a grin.

'You were supposed
to help cart this stuff
to the tree house.
What kept you?'

'Something happen?'
Tash put her boxes down more
carefully. 'You look worried.'

Elly sighed. 'Aunt Dina has an old friend
staying. She's just a bit…well. Never mind.'
She felt disloyal complaining about her aunt's
friend. 'She held me up, that's all.'

'Oh wow! I never thought I'd get to meet
an actual survivor of Boring-Grown-up-
Guest Syndrome!' Sierra's eyes were wide
with awe. 'You're totally my hero. Which
means you're forgiven.'

'And you're still in time to help.' Tash
picked up one of her boxes and shoved it into
Elly's arms.

'What's in this? It weighs a tonne.'

'All will be revealed,' Tash intoned in a
spooky voice.

3

***

'Thanks, guys.' Tash collapsed onto the floor of the tree house.

'Hey, don't damage the slave labour.' Sierra pulled her leg out of the way. She was lying near Tash on her back, groaning at the ceiling. 'I may not live. I need another doughnut, quick!' She stuck out a hand. Elly dropped a doughnut in it.

'Sorry I couldn't get here in time to help.' Elly sat cross-legged on her cushion, nibbling a doughnut and trying not to feel even more fed up with Celeste.

'Not your fault,' Tash said. 'And you did help. I didn't realize it would be such hard work but Mum is sorting through all Grandad's inventions. Some of the big ones are going to a museum, but she said I could keep some of my favourites. I wanted to get them out of the house now so they don't get mixed up with the others by mistake.'

They had pulled the boxes up to the tree house one at a time, in Mojo's dog basket lift. Tash had only just finished unpacking, and now the inside of the tree house was piled with empty boxes and crowded with strange machines made of wood, plastic, wire, and glass.

'You'll get my bill in the morning,' Sierra muttered around the last of her doughnut. 'Trust Old Man Blake's inventions to weigh a tonne. After all, a considerate person wouldn't make an open-grave-tourist-trap… Oh!' She bolted upright, her eyes wide with horror. 'I'm sorry, Tash! I keep forgetting he was your grandfather. I mean, he seems more like a story from a long time ago.'

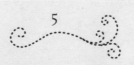

'He died when I was five.' Tash sat up. She wrapped her arms around her knees and rested her head on them, her spiky blonde hair even messier than usual.

Elly thought she looked suddenly very sad. 'Do you remember him?' she asked.

'Yes.' Tash's voice was wistful. 'I know I joke about him like everyone else, but I miss him a lot. He's almost the only thing I do remember from when I was little. I followed him around like a puppy, but he never seemed to mind. Mostly I remember being in his workshop. The rest of the house was dusty and dirty, but that room sparkled. It was full of shiny bits of metal, tiny coils of wire, boxes of screws and nuts…all sorts of tiny, delicate mechanical things. Like a factory run by fairies. And he would sit there at his table, holding these miniature screwdrivers and pliers in his big, wrinkled old hands. While he worked he told me stories about his inventions.' She paused. 'I really loved him.'

'I'm so sorry I said that about him,' Sierra mumbled.

'It's OK.' Tash shrugged. 'I'm used to people thinking Grandad was crazy. Sometimes I think he must have been too. But it was the happiest time of my life. Till I met you two!' She smiled warmly at them, all traces of sadness gone. 'I'm just glad Mum said I could have these inventions to remember him by. She wants the rest to go to a museum. Some professor is coming this week to look at them. Maybe he can figure out what they do.'

'Did your grandfather tell you stories about these?' Elly gazed at the contents of the boxes with new interest. There was something that looked like an old-fashioned electric kettle and a tall plastic tube that looked like a sort of lava lamp. Most of the inventions were boxes of plastic or wood covered in dials and switches. A few had coloured wires looping crazily over their surface. She spotted an unopened cardboard box. 'Hey, you haven't unpacked that one.'

'That one's special.' Tash jumped to her feet, opened the container and lifted out a large, heavy-looking wooden box. She placed it on the table and turned to look at them, her face solemn. 'I need you guys to help me solve a mystery.'

Chapter 2

'What mystery?' Elly asked.

'Is it in the box?' Sierra asked.

Tash turned back to the box and wiped off a layer of dust with a tissue. Dark brown wood gleamed in the light from the camping lamp. A thin line showed where the top and bottom joined, but Elly couldn't see any hinges, latch, or keyhole.

'How do you open it?'

'That's the mystery,' Tash said. 'Grandad left this box to me in his will. I've never been able to figure out how to open it. I think it's a puzzle box.'

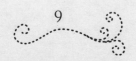

Sierra's eyes widened. 'Your grandad willed it to you? There's got to be something valuable inside: diamonds…or the deed to a gold mine!'

'A mysterious treasure box!' Elly felt the smooth wood, running her finger around the tantalizing seam. 'I wonder why he didn't leave instructions about how to open it?'

'He wanted me to figure it out,' Tash said. 'Grandad loved puzzles. Try lifting it; careful though. Whatever's inside could be delicate.'

Gingerly, Elly lifted the box in both hands. 'It's heavy.'

'Gold! I knew it! Ohh,' Sierra squealed. 'How can you bear it, Tash? I'd have to break it open.'

'No.' Tash shook her head. 'Grandad thought I was clever enough to open this box and I'm not going to cheat.'

'Let's all have a go.' Sierra touched the box. 'We've got to be cleverer than it is.'

Half an hour and half a dozen doughnuts later, she conceded defeat. 'Oh my godfathers! I'm stupider than a block of wood. That is very not funny.' She slumped back onto the floor.

'I've been trying for seven years,' Tash said with a groan.

'OK. I feel a bit better.' Sierra grinned at Tash. 'I'm boxed out though.' She turned to Elly. 'You've been too quiet all evening. You've only eaten three doughnuts, which is pathetic. Something's up. Spill.'

'Your aunt's friend?' Tash guessed.

Elly hesitated. It felt mean to complain about Celeste, but she couldn't say anything to Aunt Dina. 'The problem is…' She sighed. 'I feel really bad saying this, but I don't like her.'

'You don't have to like everyone,' Tash said.

'Not even you!' Sierra smiled at her.

Elly felt herself relax. She should have known she could trust Tash and Sierra to understand. 'It's not Celeste so much…I mean, she's a bit drippy, always wearing black like a goth even though she's way too old. She hardly ever smiles and talks in this hushed voice all the time, like everything's super-serious. You know?'

Sierra groaned. 'I've got a teacher like that. Everyone calls her "Triple D" for Dreary Droning Drip. No one pays attention in class. I can't help feeling a bit sorry for her, but it's her own fault.'

Elly nodded. 'Celeste is sort of like that, 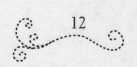 but not so bad,' she added quickly. It was important to be fair. 'But the worst thing about her is the ghosts.'

'Ghosts?' Sierra's half-

eaten doughnut paused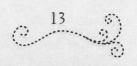
in mid-air.

'Your aunt's friend
keeps pet ghosts?' Tash's
blue eyes sparkled but her face was
serious. 'I bet dogs are easier to house train.'

An image of Celeste training a ghost to sit,
stay, and roll over flashed through Elly's head.
Giggles rose in her throat. Sierra choked and
splurted doughnut fragments. Tash gave up
pretending and roared. Mojo jumped to his
feet, barking with excitement.

'Explain!' Sierra demanded, when she was
able to speak again.

'She's a ghost hunter.'

'You're having us on.' Sierra turned to Tash.
'She's kidding, right?'

But Tash had stopped smiling. She leant
forward. 'Go on,' she urged.

'It's true,' Elly said. 'She calls herself a
medium. She says she can talk to ghosts. She
came here because apparently there have

13

been ghost sightings on Sunday Island.'

'I haven't heard about anything like that,' Sierra said. 'She must be making it up.'

'All I know is she's heard about these sightings and wants to check them out.' Elly shrugged.

'There's no such things as ghosts!' Sierra declared, pulling a stubborn face.

Tash jumped to her feet, rummaged inside the last unpacked box and lifted out a strange-looking object. It was a small plastic rectangle with a light bulb on top and a speedometer-like needle gauge on the front.

'What is that?' Sierra eyed the object warily.

Tash grinned at them. 'It's Grandad's ghost detector. Maybe we should let Celeste borrow it, Elly. It's supposed to detect paranormal activity.'

Sierra snorted. 'Seriously?

That piece of junk actually works?'

Tash shrugged. 'Some of Grandad's inventions do. I say we try this one out.'

'It can't work because there's no such things as ghosts.' Sierra was looking mutinous.

Elly didn't want an argument to spoil their sleepover. 'Then it can't hurt to try. Come on, Sierra, it's just a bit of fun.'

'OK…but I don't see the point.'

Tash put the box on the table and picked up her big emergency torch. 'We'll use the batteries from this. It runs on the same size.'

'You've tried it before?' Elly asked. 'Did it work?'

'Actually, no.' Tash slotted the batteries into the ghost detector and snapped the compartment shut. 'It just sat there.'

Sierra relaxed. 'Oh, go on, then. Turn it on.'

'Do you want to do it, Elly?' Tash asked.

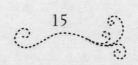

'Sure!' Elly felt butterflies fluttering in her stomach. She reached down and clicked on the switch. It looked like an ordinary light switch on a wall, but the bulb didn't light up. In fact, nothing happened at all. Elly didn't know whether to be pleased or disappointed. She glanced up at her friends.

Tash shrugged. Sierra brushed her long dark hair over her shoulder. 'See? There's no such things as—'

The gadget began to whirr. The light bulb flicked on and began to glow with an eerie blue light. The needle on the dial shuddered into life, flickering around the dial, from blue into white, edging slowly but surely towards the red.

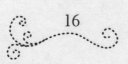

The tree house was totally silent except for the faint whirr of the ghost detector. Elly realized she had forgotten to breathe.

Sierra's face had
gone pale.

'Well.' Tash's voice
sounded ridiculously normal.
'It looks like I own a haunted tree house!'

Chapter 3

'I *still* don't believe in ghosts!' Sierra shivered and looked over her shoulder.

'Whether you believe in ghosts or not,' Tash said, 'Grandad's ghost detector says there's one near us right now.' She grinned wickedly.

'You're just trying to scare me.' Sierra fingered the bangles she wore on her left wrist, rubbing them up and down until they tinkled like wind chimes. 'But it won't work. That thing's short-circuited or something.' As if to prove her words, the ghost detector stopped whirring. The blue light faded, and the needle dropped to the bottom of the dial.

Elly flicked the switch on and off several times. Nothing happened. 'Do you think it's broken?'

'The ghost has obviously left to go haunting somewhere else,' Tash said. 'If we're lucky, it'll come back soon.'

'Lucky?' Sierra shuddered. 'Ghosts are scary—not fun.'

'How can they be scary if they don't exist?' Tash teased.

'You expect logic? At this time of night?' Sierra jumped to her feet. 'I'm putting this away: I've had enough of ghosts for now.' She took the ghost detector and headed towards the jumble of packing boxes, where Mojo was happily curled up on top of the towering pile. 'Oh no! Mojo! Get down from there!'

The dog yipped in dismay. Elly whipped

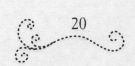

round to see the
border terrier slide
off the empty boxes
and crash into the tree
house's only lamp. It teetered,
slowly toppled over and the bulb exploded,
sending up a shower of sparks. Smoke began
to drift up from the empty boxes.

'Fire!' shrieked Sierra.

'Mojo! No!' Tash leapt up, grabbed an open
can of lemonade and threw its contents on
the boxes. The border terrier scrambled for
cover to the opposite side of the room as the
sparks hissed and died.

'Hooray!' shouted Elly. 'That's put it out.'

Tash righted the lamp. Sierra carefully
swept up the broken bits. Elly jumped to her
feet, threw the window open wide and began
to fan the smoke with a magazine, chasing it
outside. When the tree house was clear, she
paused a moment, gazing out. The island was
flooded in moonlight, a magical land washed

with silver and indigo. Then she gasped. A white light glared out of the darkness nearby, blinking like a lighthouse: on, off, on, off.

'Sierra! Tash! Come here, quickly!' Elly pointed out of the window, her head full of ghostly ideas. 'Look…'

Sierra ran to the window. 'What? I don't see anything. You've been breathing in too much smoke—' She gasped. 'No, wait. There is… something. Tash, come and look!'

'It's just someone out walking with a torch, guys. I…Oh.' Tash's voice changed as she peered out into the darkness. 'That's weird. It looks like someone signalling. Must be Morse Code. They teach it at the sailing club. Let me see if I can figure this out.'

Elly felt shivers run up and down her arms.

What had they stumbled

across? Spies?
Smugglers? Or
was it the ghosts
that Old Man
Blake's machine had
detected?

'U—S—K—R—P—J…Hang on,' Tash spelt out the letters in a hushed voice. 'That's not a word.'

'Not in English, anyway.' Sierra's voice dropped to a whisper. 'Maybe it's foreign spies!'

'On Sunday Island?' Tash laughed. 'Doubt it.'

'It has to mean something,' Elly insisted.

'Tourists? Kids playing games?' Tash suggested. 'Only…I'm sure that's coming from the graveyard. What would tourists be doing there?'

'Graveyard?' Sierra groaned. 'First your grandad's ghost detector goes off. Now there are spooky lights in the graveyard. I really don't like this.'

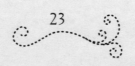

'Oh come on, Sierra!' Tash said. 'This is exciting. It looks like your aunt's friend is right, Elly. Sunday Island is haunted!'

Chapter 4

'I take it all back!' Sierra said. 'Your grandad's inventions work. But if there's a ghost in the graveyard I'm going home.'

'There could be a perfectly normal explanation,' soothed Elly. 'Remember when I found you in Old Man Blake's grave? I thought you were a ghost at first.'

Tash nodded. 'Only one way to find out.'

'No!' Sierra said, crossing her arms. 'Absolutely not!'

But Tash was already slinging on her jacket. 'Mojo, you're staying here. You've done enough damage tonight.'

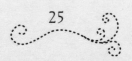

The dog whimpered, but went to sit in his basket.

'I'm sorry. But you'd scare off any ghost,' Tash told him, walking over to pat him. 'Elly, you coming? Sierra, you can stay here with Mojo if you want.'

'By myself?' Sierra looked horrified. 'Are you crazy?!' She slid into her pink denim jacket and pulled her purple handbag over her shoulder. 'But I'm bringing this.' She pulled a torch out of her bag and waved it at Tash. 'For light and protection. I can hit ghosts with it.'

Elly giggled as she tugged on her fleece. 'You can't hit ghosts. Celeste says they're made of ectoplasm or something.'

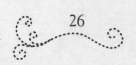

'Just don't hit us by mistake.' Tash gathered up the ghost detector. 'You're not bringing that!' Sierra protested.

'Of course I am! Don't you want to know if the graveyard is haunted?'

Sierra stared at Tash. 'I can't believe you asked me that.'

Elly grabbed her by the hand and pulled her to the trapdoor. Tash lowered the rope ladder. Mojo whined from his basket, thumping his tail on the floor hopefully.

'Sorry, Mojo,' Tash called. 'You're in charge here. Hold the fort and keep off all ghostly attackers.'

'Tell me we're not really doing this,' Sierra muttered as she swung down the ladder after Tash.

Elly didn't answer. She was too busy watching the mysterious light blinking in the distance. What could it mean? She climbed down the ladder after Sierra, the midnight air cooling her hot face, her heart thudding.

They wound through the maze, Tash taking

the lead. The moon sat above the horizon, its silver light casting sharp-edged shadows onto the ground in front of them. Over the faint scuffing noise of their footsteps, Elly could hear Sierra humming the same cheerful tune, over and over again. Just as Elly spotted the gap in the wall of the yew hedge that marked the entrance to the maze, Tash raised her hand and stopped.

'We need to sneak up,' she whispered. 'So we don't scare whoever it is off.'

'Scaring them off sounds like a good idea to me.' Sierra fidgeted with her bangles, her friendship charm shining silver in the moonlight.

Elly put a warning hand on Sierra's arm to stop the bangles clinking.

Sierra pulled her jacket sleeve down. 'Sorry!'

There was a harsh beating of wings directly overhead, followed by the screech of a hunting owl. Then silence, and Elly's heart slowed to normal.

'Only an owl,' Tash said in a shaky voice.

'Maybe it's a ghost pretending to be a bird.' Sierra laughed, nervously. 'Maybe it's warning us to stay away!'

'Maybe it's just an owl after its supper,' Elly said, giving Sierra's hand a quick squeeze. 'Come on. I want to see what was making that light.' Her stomach was more fluttery than ever, but turning back would be giving up. Her fingers found the friendship charm around her neck. It had belonged to her mother and Elly never took it off.

'So do I.' Tash patted her own friendship charm, which was pinned to her scarf.

'Or we could just forget we saw that light, go back to the tree house, eat junk and wreck some more of your grandad's inventions. That works for... *Hey!*'

Elly and Tash grabbed Sierra by the arms and pulled her after them.

The graveyard seemed empty and silent. Elly tripped on clumps of heather, her eyes straining for any sign of the mysterious light. Sierra gripped her hand so tightly Elly couldn't feel her fingers.

The light had vanished. Elly looked at Tash, who shrugged. 'Whatever it was seems to have gone,' Tash whispered.

'Can we go too?' Sierra let go of Elly's hand, tugged the strap of her handbag back on to her shoulder and hugged her denim jacket close.

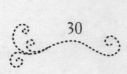

'Oh come on. Not yet.' Elly turned round to make sure of the position of the tree house. 'The light was coming from

over there.' She
pointed to a small
stone building half
buried in weeds in the
centre of the graveyard.

Two angels stood with bent heads and
drooping wings either side of a dark doorway.
Rusty wrought-iron railings surrounded the
building, spikes spearing skywards through a
tangle of brambles.

'Uew!' Sierra said. 'That's straight out of a
horror movie.'

'That's the Blake family crypt.' Tash pushed
through the overgrown bracken and brambles
tangling the older part of the graveyard. Elly
dodged after her, the brambles snagging her
jeans. Sierra followed, muttering a string of
interesting-sounding Spanish words.

When they reached the crypt, Tash took
the ghost detector from under her arm and
switched it on. Elly peered over her shoulder
at the needle on the spook-detecting dial. It

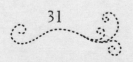

didn't move. Sierra stood a few steps away, clutching her handbag close to her chest and glancing nervously around the graveyard. 'Well?' she hissed impatiently after a few seconds. 'Is this place haunted or not?'

Tash flipped the switch off, then on again. The blue light bulb remained dark. The needle on the dial, just visible in the light of the moon, remained motionless. 'No.' Tash's voice was disappointed. 'Nothing. It's either not working or there aren't any ghosts here after all.'

'But we didn't imagine that light.' Elly frowned at the crypt, frustrated. 'And it came from right around here.'

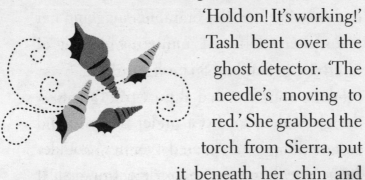

'Hold on! It's working!' Tash bent over the ghost detector. 'The needle's moving to red.' She grabbed the torch from Sierra, put it beneath her chin and

grinned ghoulishly at them. 'We are not alone.'

'That's all I need,' Sierra said, snatching back the torch. 'I wish you hadn't brought—' She broke off and stared at the far side of the crypt, a look of growing horror on her face. 'Listen!' she hissed.

Tash stared at her. 'What's the matter?' Her eyes grew wide and she turned her head slowly towards the crypt.

Now Elly could hear it. A gnawing. A scratching and scrabbling. Like a giant rat eating its way through earth and stone. And it was coming from inside the crypt.

Sierra squealed and ran, crashing out of sight through brambles and bracken. Even over the sound of her retreat, the gnawing noises from the crypt grew louder. The picture of a ghoul with steel teeth and claws rending its way out through the stone walls

flashed inside Elly's head. She grabbed Tash's hand. 'Come on!'

They bolted after Sierra together, running as fast as possible for the maze, the tree house, and safety.

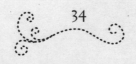

Chapter 5

Morning seagulls had replaced midnight owls as Elly walked between Sierra and Tash down the hill to Aunt Dina's cottage for breakfast. Mojo pattered ahead of them on the dusty path. The sun was already high in a cloudless sky.

Tash didn't seem to want to talk. She was frowning in thought and tugging her blonde hair into new spikes. Sierra, on the other hand, hadn't stopped chattering since they'd woken up. She seemed to be competing with the seagulls about who could make the most noise.

Elly yawned. She had lain awake in her sleeping bag for hours. Her friends looked as crumpled and washed out as she felt. Had it really been a ghost in the graveyard last night? Elly shivered at the memory of it all, then yawned again.

'Oh stop it!' Sierra groaned. 'Yawns are c-catchi—ooaaooh.'

Tash cheered up as they reached the cottage. It might have had something to do with the delicious smells that greeted them as they opened the front door.

'I totally *love* your Aunt Dina,' Sierra said fervently.

'You mean you love her cooking,' Tash teased.

'That too.' Sierra grinned. 'And don't tell me you don't because I can see you drooling.'

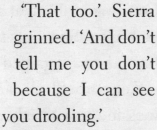

'That you, girls? Just

in time. Breakfast is in the garden this morning.' Aunt Dina's voice wafted out of the kitchen along with smells of bacon and cinnamon.

Sierra dived into the kitchen, Tash hard on her heels. Elly followed, and received her aunt's third monster hug of the day.

'Hello, love.' A flour-smudged Aunt Dina gave her a contented smile. She loved cooking and Elly could tell she was pleased with the results. She raised her eyebrows at Elly. 'You're the third bedraggled, sleepy little mouse the old cat dragged in this morning. Ought to be called "wake-overs", not "sleep-overs". Never mind. A good breakfast will put you right.' She waved them through into the tiny courtyard garden behind the cottage.

Celeste was already sitting at the pretty mosaic table. Elly's heart sank as she saw her aunt's friend. The excitement last night had almost made her forget Celeste. Don't be mean! she told herself, and slipped into a chair between Tash and Sierra.

Aunt Dina's visitor was wearing a floaty black skirt beneath a droopy jumper. Silver chains strewn with crystals dangled from her neck and her fingers were almost hidden beneath thick rings engraved with strange marks and patterns. She gazed around the table at them, her green eyes ringed with black eyeliner.

'How lovely to meet Elly's friends at last.' Celeste smiled at Tash and Sierra. 'I was over the moon when Dee told me you were joining us for breakfast.'

'Dig in!' Aunt Dina lowered a plate piled high with American-style French toast, next to a platter of bacon. 'I know three hungry girls when I see them.'

'Mmmm.' When Elly looked up at last from her plate, she saw two dreamy smiles on her friends' faces and could feel another spread across her own. Tash slid the last piece of toast onto her plate and smothered it with butter and maple syrup, and Sierra was delicately holding the last piece of bacon between two fingers, taking mouse-sized nibbles to make it last and looking as contented as Mojo, who lounged beneath the table munching dog treats. He was thumping his tail in approval. If Sierra had a tail, Elly thought, she would be doing the same.

'That was great.' Tash drained the last of her hot chocolate and beamed at Aunt Dina. 'Food never tastes this good anywhere else. You should start a restaurant.'

'Oh no,' Aunt Dina laughed. 'That would turn making good food into work. Painting for a living and cooking for fun suits me just fine. And at least the three of you are looking a bit livelier. Tough night, was it?'

'You've no idea.' Sierra groaned. 'I couldn't sleep at all after the ghost in the graveyard.'

Celeste sat bolt upright in her chair.

'Ghosts?' Aunt Dina laughed. Her voice sank to a spooky whisper: 'By Haunts and All-Hallows and Things that Go Bump in the Night, I think you've been talking to Celeste.'

'Really, Dee!' The medium sighed. 'You never take these things seriously enough.'

Reluctantly, Elly explained about the mysterious light and the trip to the graveyard.

'But how exciting!' Celeste exclaimed. She stared across the table at Elly, pinning her with a mascara-ringed gaze. Her husky voice became even more intense and

soulful. 'You say
the light flashed
on and off, as though
someone — or something —
was attempting to signal?'

Elly just nodded. The more Celeste asked questions, the less Elly felt like answering them. Her aunt's friend twisted round to lean at Tash next, who blinked and edged her chair away. 'Can you describe these sounds you heard coming from your family crypt?'

'It sounded like scratching or digging,' Tash said. 'But it wasn't an animal. It was too loud for that.'

'Exciting!' Celeste fingered her crystal-strewn necklaces, gazing at all of them in turn. 'I have come to Sunday Island because it has a reputation for being haunted. Ghosts of soldiers who died in World War Two, digging the tunnels beneath the island. That, of course, would explain the digging noise you heard.'

'Except,' Sierra said, 'there's no such things as ghosts.'

'A sceptic!' Celeste smiled indulgently.

'To be honest,' Sierra said with a shrug, 'I'm scared of anything spooky, so I'd rather they didn't exist. But I also think that if there were ghosts, scientists would have found out about them by now.'

'Not everything in life can be explained through science,' Aunt Dina added. 'At least not yet. For which I'm grateful. I like there to be a few mysteries left.'

'Do you believe in ghosts?' Elly frowned at her aunt. A new thought had jumped into her head. She wasn't sure she believed in ghosts. At least, she didn't think she did. And if ghosts did exist, was there a way to talk to them? Elly's mum had died of cancer earlier

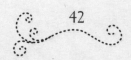

in the year, and the idea of being able to talk to her mother, just once more, twisted Elly's stomach up into a hard knot. She stared at her plate, blinking back sudden tears and trying not to let Aunt Dina see that she was upset.

But her aunt was busy gathering up the breakfast plates. 'I neither believe nor disbelieve. I prefer to keep my mind open.'

'I wonder,' Celeste began. 'Dee, I've had a brilliant idea. What do you think about holding a séance? Would you let me have one here, in the cottage? Perhaps a medium such as me will be able to communicate with the spirits that linger on Sunday Island, and we can find out who they are and what troubles them.'

'That's a great idea!' Tash's eyes widened with excitement.

'Would your mother like to come?' Aunt Dina asked. 'And what about your father, Sierra? After all, he's researching the tunnels isn't he? We might as well have a bit of a party while we're at it. I'd enjoy cooking a pre-séance meal.'

'Oh,' Tash's face fell. 'I suppose I could ask her. And there's a historian who's come to value Grandad's inventions for the museum. He could talk to your dad about the tunnels, Sierra.'

'Dad would love to come, especially if you're cooking one of your scrummy meals, Dina. But I think I'll skip it.' Sierra shuddered. 'One spooky night a week is enough for me.'

'Oh, don't spoil it, Sierra!' Tash cried. 'How are we going to solve the mystery if we stay at home with the covers over our

heads? Right Elly?'

Both her friends turned to look at her. Oh, don't ask me to decide, Elly thought. I don't really believe in Celeste or her séances. Part of her was certain that if her mother really wanted to talk to her, this wouldn't be the way it would happen. But Tash looked so keen. Elly didn't want to let her down.

Sierra shrugged. 'I'll come if you do, Elly,' she said. 'Don't want to be a party-pooper.'

'Oh, do say yes, Elly,' Celeste pleaded. 'I can sense that the spirits will favour us.'

'Only if you want to.' Aunt Dina was watching her now, her eyes suddenly sharp. 'If you'd rather not—'

'No. No, it's fine,' Elly said quickly. 'A séance.' She smiled at them all. 'Great.'

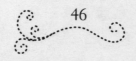

Chapter 6

Elly perched on an outcrop of granite on the hillside, waiting. She had decided to escape the craziness of Aunt Dina's cottage for a rendezvous with Tash and Sierra. Celeste was swooping around like a dizzy bat, preparing for the evening's séance, and Aunt Dina's cottage overflowed with floaty scarves, smelly candles, and dangling crystals. It was much more peaceful here, sitting above the graveyard in the bright sunlight.

Elly spotted Tash first, her spiky blonde head bobbing along the path from Sunday House, Mojo trotting at her heels. Cheerful

whistling floated up on the breeze.

It had been Tash's idea to investigate the graveyard in daylight. Sierra on the other hand…There she was now: stalking along the path from the caravan park; head hanging down, long dark hair hiding her face. It had taken all Tash's pleading and teasing to get her to agree to come back here.

Elly bounded to her feet and waved to attract Tash's attention. Mojo ran up, his tail rotating like a propeller with excitement.

Tash's eyes were glowing. 'Ready for some ghost detecting? Look what I brought.' She opened her backpack and Elly glimpsed Old Man Blake's ghost detector.

'I might have known.' Sierra strolled up to them.

Tash smiled at Sierra. 'Thanks for coming. It wouldn't be the same without you.'

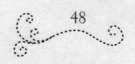

Sierra shook her head. 'You mean without someone squeaking at every spooky noise. I know I'm a wimp.'

'You're braver than either of us,' Elly said. 'You're scared but you came anyway.'

They negotiated the bramble patches guarding the Blake family crypt, picking ripe, luscious blackberries as they went. With the sun beating down and her mouth full of blackberry juice, Elly couldn't quite believe that last night had happened. A fat speckled thrush scratched in the undergrowth. The faint hum of crickets filled the air. Bees lazed slowly among the purple and orange heather blossom. It was a perfect summer day on Sunday Island.

Tash sighed. 'Not very ghostly today, is it?'

'What a relief,' Sierra said around a mouthful of blackberries. Her hands and lips were stained purple. 'Right, Mojo?'

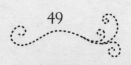

But the dog had pricked up his ears. He gave a sharp excited bark and scrambled through the undergrowth ahead of them, heading right for the crypt.

'Mojo!' Tash raced after him.

'Now what?' Sierra dumped her handful of berries. Elly shrugged and jogged after Tash. Brambles scratched her legs, making her wish she'd worn jeans instead of shorts.

Tash's voice rang out. 'Mojo! No! Come back!'

Elly pushed through into the clearing around the crypt, Sierra close behind. Tash was standing frozen outside the tomb. Elly's heart gave a thud when she saw why.

The metal door to the Blake family crypt stood half open, showing a dark tunnel-like opening leading underground.

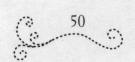

'Who opened that?' Elly stared at the rusty iron door, feeling shivers running up and down her spine.

'I've no idea.' Tash frowned, looking worried and a bit scared. 'I've never seen it open. But Mojo darted in there, so I'm going in too.'

Sierra grabbed Tash's arm. 'You can't. This has something to do with those spooky lights and that horrible noise!'

'I'm not leaving Mojo.' Tash shrugged off Sierra's hand.

Elly peered through the opening. Steep stone steps led down into the shadows. Her stomach was flipping over at the idea of going inside the crypt, but she knew they had to find Mojo, and she also wanted to find out what had caused the strange noises they had heard here. 'Come on.' She headed for the door, ignoring Sierra's hiss of indrawn breath.

'Wait!' Sierra stepped in front of her. 'Let

me go first. I've got a torch on my phone.' As she squeezed past, Elly could feel her shaking. She paused to pull out her own phone and turn on the torch function.

'Thanks, guys,' Tash said, following close behind. Their footsteps echoed on the stone stairs as they climbed down into the darkness. Elly's eyes strained to make out shapes. The open door cast a grey gloom near the entrance, but the rest of the crypt remained invisible.

They reached the bottom of the stairs, the light from their phones slicing through the wall of dark in narrow pencil-beams. Tash called for Mojo, but there was no response.

They flashed their torchlight around the room. White light zigzagged up, down and sideways, revealing the long grey rectangle of a heavy stone sarcophagus.

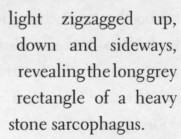

'What is that?' Sierra's

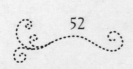

torchlight was
quivering. 'Is
that a…a coffin?'

'Sort of,' Tash said.

'Euww…vampire time.' Sierra
gave a shaky laugh.

The sarcophagus had a heavy stone lid
covered in thick dust and cobwebs. Elly
sighed with relief and her heart shifted down
a gear. The dust on the lid was undisturbed.
Whew! she thought. That sarcophagus can't
have been opened for ages. She shone her
torch around the rest of the room.

'Oh my godfathers!' Sierra's torch had
zeroed in on the same object. In the crossfire
of two beams of halogen, a stone angel reared
out of the darkness in front of them. A face
stared through draperies of tattered cobwebs
and grime, the eyes blank ovals. Its wings flared
from its back as though about to take flight.

'Mojo! Here, boy!' Tash's voice echoed
around the crypt, making Elly jump. At last

there was an answering bark, and the sound of pattering paws. 'You silly dog!' Tash knelt and scooped up the border terrier.

'Shhhh!' Elly hissed. She strained her ears. Had she imagined it? No. There it was again: footsteps, outside in the graveyard! 'Someone's coming!' she whispered, turning off her phone. 'Put out the torch, Sierra!'

Sierra gasped, but her torchlight clicked out. The crypt was completely dark now, except for the shaft of sunlight slanting through the half-open door. The air seemed suddenly hot and heavy. The sound of Elly's heart thudded in her ears...

'What if they come inside?' Tash muttered.

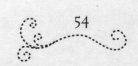

'Shhhh!' Elly listened hard. But the footsteps had stopped. Had the intruder gone away?

A hand reached out and grabbed Elly's

arm. It was freezing cold and she nearly screamed, thinking of the stone angel. 'Look!' Sierra's voice hissed through the darkness. 'The door's closing. We'll be trapped!'

Elly's scream caught in her throat. Sierra was right. The crack of light from the entrance was narrowing. They were about to be trapped inside the crypt!

'Run for it!' Tash shouted.

Elly's body seemed to have been waiting for Tash's words. She exploded into action, sprinting for the light. If that door shut they would be locked inside the tomb, and no one would think of looking for them here. They would be buried alive!

The last inch of light was disappearing in a narrow slit as she slammed into the door, shoving it with both hands. The door hit something, then sprang wide. Elly tumbled

out into the open, crashing onto her knees. Before she could stand up, Tash piled on top of her, knocking her flat. Mojo seemed to be everywhere, yipping furiously. Last of all, Sierra barrelled out of the crypt, shrieking like a banshee.

Sierra stopped in mid-scream. 'Hey. Who are you?'

'I didn't mean to shut you in,' said a frightened voice. 'I didn't know you were in there. Honest.'

Elly crawled to her feet, blinking in the glare of full sunlight.

A boy of about ten was backing slowly away from them. 'Y-you really s-scared me! I...I thought you were zombies or something coming out of that crypt like that.' He was thin, dressed in shorts

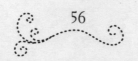

and a T-shirt, with mouse-brown hair, knobbly knees, and a slender, freckled face. He looked frightened to death, and Elly couldn't help feeling sorry for him.

'What are you doing here?' she asked.

He kept glancing about nervously, his eyes flicking left and right. 'I'm visiting the island with my uncle. I'm exploring, that's all. I saw that big old tomb was open and I thought I ought to shut the door. You know, so no animals get trapped in there. He looked at Mojo, who had stopped barking and was panting happily, Tash's hand gripping his collar. 'That's a nice dog,' he said wistfully. 'What's his name?'

'Mojo,' Tash said. 'Will someone close the crypt door, so I can let him loose? I don't want him going in again.'

Sierra pushed the metal door shut, and Tash released Mojo. The border terrier immediately ran to investigate the boy, who squatted and put his hand out for Mojo to sniff. 'Can I pet him?' He glanced at Tash hopefully.

'Sure.' She looked at Elly and Sierra and shrugged. Elly shrugged back. The kid seemed harmless enough. Mojo certainly liked him, and Tash always claimed he had a sixth sense about people. Elly relaxed. Their mysterious intruder was just a kid on holiday. But she still shuddered at the thought of how close they had come to being trapped inside the crypt.

'What's your name?' Sierra asked.

'Russell.' The boy was scratching Mojo behind the ears. He looked up, a shy smile spreading across his face. 'He's lovely, your dog.' He sighed. 'My parents won't let me have one. My dad's allergic.'

'That's a shame,' Tash said.

'I've had a brilliant idea,' Elly said. Russell was looking more relaxed, but Elly felt bad about the scare they'd given him. And their near escape deserved celebration. 'Why don't we all go to town for an ice cream? You come too, Russell.'

'Genius!' Sierra licked her lips. 'I'm starving. Terror does that to me.'

'Everything does that to you.' Tash turned to Russell. 'It's good ice cream, though. You wanna come?'

The boy blushed. 'Haven't got any money.' He gave Mojo a last pat and stood up. 'Thanks anyway.'

'We'll treat you,' Tash said. 'Mojo'll have one too, won't you, boy?' The border terrier gave an approving bark and trotted away at once in the direction of town.

'I guess that's yes.' Russell grinned at them.

As they made their way down to the town, Russell chattered away, telling them about his favourite computer games. It seemed as if he was over his fright now.

The high street was crowded with day-trippers from the mainland. Sensing where they were heading, Mojo darted off in the direction of the ice cream parlour. Sierra raced after him, with Tash hard on their heels.

'He's not very well trained,' Russell observed to Elly. 'But some of the clever breeds are like that. I saw this programme about it on TV. They only obey you when they want to.' His eyes were glued to Mojo, and Elly found herself hoping he got his dog some day. Then she saw his face stiffen and his smile drain away. He was looking at something else now, just ahead of them. Elly turned to look,

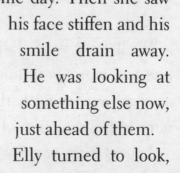

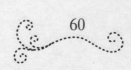

but there was nothing except a pavement full of tourists. A family with four screaming little kids bustled through the crowd, the parents red-faced and sweating. A tall man in a hot-looking tweed suit pushed by.

She turned back to ask Russell what was wrong. But the boy had vanished. Elly stood in the middle of the busy street, twisting around for a sight of him, unable to believe he'd disappeared without his ice cream or even saying goodbye. The boy from the graveyard was gone.

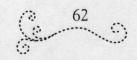

Chapter 7

Mojo was not enjoying himself. Elly wasn't either, but she was doing her best not to let on. Aunt Dina had gone to masses of trouble to make the spooky evening special. Her aunt had made her famous spicy sausage casserole for dinner, and the girls had helped make chocolate raspberry ripple cheesecake for dessert.

Eight of them sat around the dining room table. Tash and her mum had brought the historian from London, Professor Partlow, who was valuing Old Man Blake's inventions. With his large head, lanky legs, and long feet in pointed shoes, the professor looked like a stork dressed in brown tweed. Elly had recognized him at once—it was the man she had seen earlier that day in town, when they went for ice cream with Russell. Before he had disappeared into the crowd.

Elly ate a forkful of sausage and rice and glanced across the table at Sierra. Her friend was watching her father and wincing. Mr Cruz was writing a book on the network of tunnels dug beneath Sunday Island during World War Two. He had spent the whole dinner quarrelling with Professor Partlow about island history.

'I think you are mistaken.' The professor frowned at Mr Cruz, his high-pitched voice growing more and more insistent. 'I would advise you to broaden your research. Hearsay and gossip are hardly conclusive. There is no documented evidence that Sunday Island played a significant role in wartime espionage efforts, or indeed, any part in the war effort at all.'

'Then why would a cash-strapped government spend money digging all those tunnels?' Mr Cruz snapped, his plump face pink and earnest. Sierra rolled her eyes in embarrassment and Elly gave her a sympathetic glance.

Mojo whimpered. He probably didn't like the prickly atmosphere either. Elly slipped a piece of sausage off her plate and wiggled it at him under the table. A whiskery nose investigated her fingers and invisible teeth delicately snapped up the offering. She felt the dog settle beside her, leaning on her legs, his tail thumping happily on the floor.

If only a bit of sausage could cheer me up,

Elly thought. But the closer the séance came, the more she disliked the idea of it. Ghosts seemed to be a game to Tash and Sierra, and even to Celeste, in a way. But whenever Elly thought of her mother, tonight felt all wrong. People being dead is not a game, she whispered to herself, and reached down to stroke Mojo. He licked her hand, and she felt a bit better.

'Gentlemen!' Celeste interrupted the history debate. 'Perhaps our ghostly visitors will be able to solve the mystery of why the tunnels were built.'

'Nonsense!' snapped Professor Partlow.

Celeste straightened from her habitual droop, looking like an offended bat. Tash's mum hid a smile in her napkin, and Sierra's dad snorted in unwilling sympathy.

'More cheesecake, Mr Cruz?' Aunt Dina said quickly. 'Professor Partlow, have you had enough? Yes? Then, girls, would you please clear away? We'll have coffee in the sitting room, I think.' She rose to her feet.

Elly jumped up, eager to get out of the room for a few moments. Tash and Sierra grabbed plates and cutlery and headed for the kitchen. As Elly followed, she heard Celeste speak, her voice throaty with irritation: 'Could everyone please wait in the sitting room. I need to clear this room of negative energy before the séance can commence.'

'Wow,' breathed Sierra, when the kitchen door was safely shut behind them. 'Negative energy is right. I thought my dad was going to punch the professor.'

Elly frowned, putting leftovers in the fridge. 'Maybe we should forget about this séance.'

'Oh, come on, Elly.' Tash turned round,

wiping her hands on a towel. 'We've put up with all that fighting; let's have some fun now.'

Elly didn't want to argue. She followed her friends into the sitting room. But Mojo headed to the dining room door instead and began to growl.

'Mojo! What's got into you?' Tash ran to pull him away.

'I suppose he's a sceptic too,' her mother said with a laugh.

'Perhaps this wasn't such a good idea.' Aunt Dina cast a worried glance at the dining room door. Elly could hear strange noises from inside: bumps and faint thuds. What was Celeste doing in there?

'Don't worry, Dina,' Mrs Blake-Reynolds said. 'You've given us a lovely dinner, and I've never been to a séance before. I've no idea what to expect.'

'Tom-foolery of some sort,' Professor Partlow said. He snorted in derision. 'Still, the belief in ghosts is a curious if trivial historical phenomenon. I shall be interested to observe a modern incarnation of the ancient practices of ghost calling. And your dinner was indeed delicious, Miss Valentine.' He inclined his head in a stiff little bow.

'I gave up on designing a ghostly menu,' Aunt Dina said with a laugh. 'All I could come up with was white food, so you've been saved from a dinner of potato soup and rice pudding.'

The door to the dining room sprang open. Celeste, a black and purple shawl pulled over her head like a hooded cloak, gestured silently for them to enter. Mojo growled. Tash had been sitting cross-legged on the floor, holding the dog on her lap, but now the small ruff of fur around the border terrier's neck stood up like a lion's mane. A shiver trickled down Elly's spine. Did Mojo sense some unseen presence?

'Shush, Mojo, don't be rude.' Tash stood and led the way into the dining room, the border terrier trotting at her heels and growling softly. Sierra followed more slowly, glancing at her father to make sure he was coming.

Mr Cruz heaved himself out of his chair. 'I've eaten too much of your good food,' he said to Aunt Dina. 'I fear the séance will give me indigestion.'

'In that case, we'll ask Celeste to produce a soothing spirit.' Aunt Dina ushered her guests into the dining room. Elly hesitated, then walked slowly into the dining room after the others, aware of her stomach squirming like a tangle of worms.

The room was transformed. Long drifts of gauzy fabric

were draped like shrouds over the furniture. Crystals dangled from the ceiling and twisted on ribbons in the curtained window. The only light came from a single fat candle sitting in the middle of the dining table. It gave off a strong perfume that reminded Elly of cat litter and room freshener.

'Euuew!' Sierra held her nose. 'That stinks. My eyes are watering.'

'Sierra! *Silencio!*' But Mr Cruz was obviously trying not to breathe in himself.

'It is a cleansing perfume,' Celeste said huffily. 'It contains frankincense.'

Mojo began to dash around the room, barking and growling.

'Go away, you silly dog!' Celeste snapped. 'Please,' she said to Tash. 'Take the animal outside. His presence is ruining the atmosphere.'

'Not as much as that candle,' Tash muttered. But she carried Mojo out and shut the door behind him.

'Please,' intoned Celeste. 'Seat yourselves. Join hands to complete the circle.'

Elly slipped into a chair between her two friends, and took their hands. Tash's was warm, but Sierra's felt as chilly as her own. Elly gave it an encouraging squeeze.

'Close your eyes.' Celeste's voice moaned through the room. Think only positive thoughts. Welcome the spirits!'

Elly suddenly found it hard not to giggle. This was crazy. But she dutifully closed her eyes and tried to concentrate.

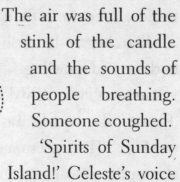

The air was full of the stink of the candle and the sounds of people breathing. Someone coughed. 'Spirits of Sunday Island!' Celeste's voice

boomed out of
the darkness. Elly
jumped. 'Spirits! Come
to us! We would speak with you.
We wish you only good things.'

Silence fell. Then...

Laughter trickled around the room. For a terrifying moment, Elly thought it was a spirit, until she realized Sierra had got a fit of nervous giggles.

'Be quiet, Sierra!' Celeste snapped. 'Welcome, good spirits!' Celeste's voice had changed. It sounded deeper, happier. 'I sense your presence. You are near...very near. Come in peace and good will. We would talk with you. Come to us, spirits!'

Elly's neck felt cold, as though someone was breathing down her back. This was getting too creepy. She opened one eye and peered around the room. Tash and Sierra were spying too. Tash winked at her. Sierra shrugged, looking freaked out. Her hand was chillier than ever. Elly darted a glance at Celeste. The medium sat straight up in her chair, droopy no longer. Her face was glowing with happiness and anticipation. She was panting like a runner at the end of a long race. As Elly watched her, fear puddled in her stomach. Something was going to happen. She could feel it.

The curtains flapped violently. The window crashed open and a cold breeze swept through the room, shivering the fabrics draped from the ceiling, making the dangling crystals clink. The candle went out and the room was plunged in darkness.

There was a moment of shocked silence as the curtains beat against the wall like giant bird wings. Then Sierra screamed.

Chapter 8

'Silence!' Celeste's voice rang out, cutting off Sierra in mid-shriek. 'Do not break the circle! No one is in danger. A spirit is here. It is a good spirit. Calm yourselves.'

Elly had given up all pretence of keeping her eyes shut. She looked at Sierra, who was sitting very still. The curtains had settled, the chilly wind had dropped. Aunt Dina was sitting straight up, tall and commanding, frowning at Celeste. Elly could tell she was wondering whether or not to put an end to the séance. But before her aunt could do anything, Celeste spoke again.

'Spirit, tell us who you are,' she crooned. 'We are here to help you. Tell us your name. Identify yourself, O spirit who walks amongst the living.' The curtain began to sway and dance, even though there was no wind. Elly felt another shiver run up and down her back.

'When did you live on Sunday Island? What binds you to this spot, wandering between life and death, unable to rest? Let us help you!'

Celeste's voice faded. The curtain stopped moving. Elly could hear the sound of her own breathing, harsh in her ears. Her heart was thudding fast.

A noise rang out. It sounded like someone knocking on a door. Sierra moaned softly, and Elly squeezed her hand again.

'Have you got something to say, spirit?' Celeste's voice was low, throbbing with excitement. 'Give us your message. Tell us why you are here!'

Like the sound of waves lapping on a distant shore, a murmur filled the room. Was she really hearing it? Yes. A deep, whispering voice, breathing the same word over and over. It grew louder, but Elly couldn't make out what it was saying. Sierra clutched her hand with vice-like fingers. Elly could feel everyone in the room straining to hear the word being whispered. Louder. Louder. And then, at last, Elly heard it clearly:

'…beware…beware…BEWARE…'

The lights flashed on. Elly blinked.

Mrs Blake-Reynolds stood beside the door, her hand on the light switch. 'It's late,' she said calmly to a dazed-looking Celeste. 'Well past Natasha's bedtime. And mine, for that matter. I have an early conference call in the morning. Dina, thank you for an…

unforgettable evening. Perhaps you and the girls could come to us soon? A picnic on the beach might be pleasant.' She smiled warmly at Aunt Dina. 'Come on, Natasha. Collect Mojo. We're going home now.'

'Oh Mum!' Tash moaned. 'It was just getting exciting. Who was the spirit, Celeste? Do you know?'

'No,' Celeste said. She was massaging her forehead, looking tired and pale. 'But it was a strong visitation. A powerful personality. And I had a vision. Of an open grave.'

Sierra gasped. Mrs Blake-Reynolds glanced sharply at Celeste.

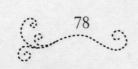

'Grandad!' Tash cried. 'It must have been him!'

'Don't be silly,' her mother snapped. 'There are no such things as ghosts.'

'It has to be him, Mum. Nothing

else makes sense.
Grandad's trying to
tell us something.
Maybe…Maybe he
doesn't want you to get
rid of his inventions.'

'Superstition and nonsense!' Professor
Partlow stood up. 'Delightful evening, Miss
Valentine. I mean, a bit of fun, but that's all,
right? Nothing serious…'

'Inventions?' Sierra's dad bounced to
his feet as well. 'Sierra, you didn't tell me
about Mr Blake's inventions. It could be of
importance to my history of the island. What
sort of inventions did your father make, Mrs
Blake-Reynolds? Did they have anything to
do with the war effort?'

'No, no,' Tash's mum shook her head
dismissively. 'My father was an eccentric.
When my mother died, he became quite odd
and spent the rest of his life making strange
machines. No one knows what most of them

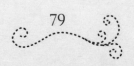

are supposed to do. And hardly any of them actually work.'

'That's not true!' Tash cried. 'The ghost detector works. We tried it out the other night and—'

'Ghost detector?' Celeste's voice rose over the general hubbub. Silence fell and everyone turned to stare at her. Her face was shiny, her mascara smudged into dark circles beneath her eyes, making her look more like a vampire than ever. 'Your grandfather invented a ghost detector? And it works? I must see it, Tash. Do you have it with you?'

'No, I…' Tash began.

'I'm sorry.' Mrs Blake-Reynolds strode forward and took Tash by the hand. 'We are going now. Goodnight.' She pulled Tash out of the door, calling for Mojo.

'I want to go home

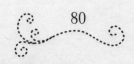

80

too, Dad.' Sierra gave Elly a quick goodbye hug, then darted over to her father and tugged him towards the door. 'I've had enough of spooks and séances for a lifetime.'

'Goodbye, Mr Cruz, Sierra. It was lovely to see you…' Aunt Dina swooped after her departing guests, finding handbags and jackets and seeing them to the door. Professor Partlow, red-faced and tweedy, stood glaring absent-mindedly at Celeste, then harrumphed and stamped out of the room without even saying goodbye.

Elly watched him leave, then turned round to say goodnight to Celeste. Her aunt's friend was shoving something into a pocket, and when she caught Elly watching her, her doughy face turned a gentle pink. That's odd, Elly thought. She looks as if I've caught her in the act. But what act? More Celeste weirdness. Elly shrugged.

'I'll close the window, shall I?' Elly strode over to pull the curtains.

'No! Don't bother! I…'

Elly grabbed the curtains and the palm of her hand was creased painfully. She looked down and saw fishing wire attached to the curtain. Celeste was clattering across the room towards her. Elly let go of the curtain as though it burnt her, her head a whirl. So that was how the curtains had moved. Trickery! Celeste was nothing but a fake! And the thing she'd hidden in her pocket must be part of it.

Elly turned round and stared at her aunt's friend, who came to a halt just in front of her. The medium was looking at her warily. She doesn't know if I found it or not, Elly thought. Maybe she should tell Aunt

Dina what she had discovered. But there was one more thing Elly wanted to find out first.

'I'm tired,' she said. She gathered up all her acting skill and smiled at Celeste. 'Goodnight.'

Celeste seemed to relax. 'Goodnight, Elly. I hope it wasn't too scary for you. Such a strong presence.'

'A bit scary,' Elly said. 'But I'm so tired I expect I'll sleep anyway. Goodnight.' As she walked past Celeste towards the door, she pretended to stumble and fell against the medium. A smartphone tumbled out of Celeste's pocket and crashed to the floor.

Elly dived for the phone. As she pretended to retrieve it, she tapped the screen to see which app had been used last.

A whispering voice filled the air: '…beware …beware…beware…'

Celeste snatched the phone out of Elly's hands. 'I recorded the spirit.' She stopped the playback and returned the phone to her pocket. 'I need to study the recording. And I'll also put it on my website for the benefit of other spiritualists. This is precious research material and I don't want a child playing with it, thank you!'

'Playing with what?' Aunt Dina strolled in to the room, yawning. 'Is there a problem?'

'No.' Celeste frowned at Elly. 'Not if I can be left alone now to recover from a strenuous session. And I must clear this room of any traces of spiritual activity, or our ghostly visitor will be drawn back to this spot.'

'By all means,' Aunt Dina said, raising her eyebrows. 'I don't fancy a haunted cottage. Come to bed, Elly, and leave Celeste to her work.'

Elly stared at her aunt, then frowned at Celeste. The medium's excuse for the recording didn't sound convincing, and there was no explanation for the wire attached to the curtains. She was a fraud—Elly knew it. But she didn't want to be the one to tell Aunt Dina. Not until she had more evidence.

Elly kissed her aunt goodnight and ran up the stairs to the attic, chased by new thoughts and questions. Sunday Island was suddenly full of strangeness. First the lights in the graveyard...Elly slid to a stop on the stairs. Whoa! What if it had been Celeste in the graveyard the other night? All the spooky stuff started *after* she showed up on Sunday Island. But if Celeste was behind the lights, what was she up to?

Elly began to slowly climb the stairs again. She had something else to worry about. Whether Celeste was behind the weirdness in the graveyard or not, she was definitely a fake. How could Elly break the news to Tash that her grandfather's ghost was nothing but a hoax?

Chapter 9

The next morning Elly awoke to a barking alarm.

Barking?

Elly sat up in bed. That was definitely Mojo's bark. It sounded as if he was outside the front door of the cottage. She checked her mobile. It was only seven a.m. What was Mojo doing here? He and Tash should still be sound asleep after the late night. She slid out of bed and slipped down the loft ladder. Aunt Dina's bedroom door was still firmly shut. Best stop Mojo barking before he woke her too.

The border terrier whined a greeting as Elly opened the front door. He trotted up and put his front paws on her legs. Elly gave him a quick pat and looked for the message he was bound to be carrying. Yes, there it was, in a leather tube attached to his collar with Velcro. Elly slid out the message and unrolled it. Tash had written the note in glittery purple ink and huge letters.

EMERGENCY MEETING
Place: Sunday House
Time: NOW!!!

Elly slipped the note back into the tube and reattached it to Mojo's collar. The dog gave her a quick, whiskery lick of thanks and raced off in the direction of

the caravan park. Sierra was about to be woken out of her sweet dreams.

Elly dashed upstairs to change into shorts and T-shirt. She put on her green flip-flops even though she could run faster in trainers. She checked to make sure her friendship charm was still safe on its chain around her neck, then wrote a quick note to Aunt Dina, explaining where she was going. She left it on the kitchen table and let herself out of the cottage.

Soon she was loping up the hill that dominated the centre of Sunday Island, heading towards Sunday House. It was a glorious morning, the sun already warming the breeze off the sea. She heard seagulls and the ever-present sound of waves slapping on pebbled beaches. In the distance the white granite cliffs and cream-coloured beaches of the mainland glowed in the sunlight, the sea sparkling cobalt.

It was impossible to feel gloomy on a morning like this. She felt crammed full of the sights and smells, the lights and colours of Sunday Island. And the sheer joy of running. But all the while, in the back of her mind she was worrying about Tash, and what the message could mean.

When Tash pulled open the front door of Sunday House and Elly saw her white, tired face she knew that it was bad news. 'What's wrong, Tash?'

'I'll tell you both.' Tash pointed behind her and Elly turned to see Sierra come charging up the path, pink flip-flops slapping.

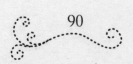

Sierra panted to a halt. 'Got here as soon as I could.'

Elly stared at her friend in concern. It looked as if Tash wasn't the only one who was upset. Sierra's eyes were swollen and red. 'Hey! Are you OK?'

Sierra reached down and fiddled with her friendship charm, which was half-hidden among the armful of bangles she always wore. 'I overheard my dad on the phone last night. I couldn't sleep what with all the spooky stuff going round my head. And you can hear every word anyone says in that caravan. Anyway, he was talking to my mum.' She smiled a watery smile. 'They're talking a lot more recently. It's sorta nice. But this wasn't. He said he doesn't think he's going to be able to sell his book on island history after all. And if he can't, he'll have to sell the caravan and leave Sunday Island for good. And I can't stay here without him.' Sierra's eyes welled with tears as she looked at them. Elly had never seen her look so miserable.

'He can't just give up.' Tash looked offended. 'We'll help him find a new publisher. I mean, how hard can it be?'

'Pretty hard, apparently,' Sierra said and shrugged. 'But I don't want to talk about it any more. We can't fix it. Why did you send Mojo this morning? What's up with you?'

'Last night I couldn't sleep either,' Tash said.

'Tell me about it,' Sierra sighed. 'Talk about nightmares. No more séances for me!'

'No.' Tash shook her head. 'It wasn't that. There were noises all night. Bumps. Thuds. When there shouldn't have been noises. Everyone had gone to bed.'

'You were dreaming,' Sierra snorted. 'What did I tell you? That séance was enough to freak anyone out.'

'I wasn't dreaming!' Tash said. 'I was wide awake most of the night. In fact, I got out

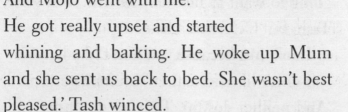

of bed and tried to find out where the noises were coming from. And Mojo went with me. He got really upset and started whining and barking. He woke up Mum and she sent us back to bed. She wasn't best pleased.' Tash winced.

'Hmmm.' Sierra frowned. 'OK, I believe you. There were scary noises in the night. What do you think they were?'

'My grandad.'

'What?' Elly stared at Tash in disbelief. And then growing dread. She would have to tell Tash about Celeste. Tash thought the spirit had been real!

'I'm sure it was my grandad's ghost at the séance last night,' Tash said. 'Why else would Celeste get a vision of an open grave? It must have been his.'

'But—' Elly began.

'Now he's haunting Sunday House. He's

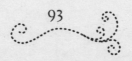

trying to tell me something!'

'Tash, that wasn't your grandad last night,' Elly said, as firmly as she could. Tash wasn't going to want to hear any of this. 'I'm sorry, Tash, but Celeste is a fake.'

'Look, just because you don't like her—'

'I don't like her either,' Sierra interrupted. 'And neither do you, Tash, so don't pretend. She's a drip.' She crossed her arms. 'Have you got proof, Elly?'

Elly nodded. 'She had a fishing line attached to the window curtain. And probably another on the catch to the window, to pull it open at the right moment. I found the wire on the curtain last night when I went to shut the window. She doesn't know I found it. But she does know I found a smartphone in her pocket—'

'In her pocket?'

Sierra goggled. 'You
picked her pocket?
You are beyond cool!'

'It was an accident,
sort of. I bumped into her
and it fell out.' Elly felt her face
grow red. 'The phone played a recording
of the voice we heard last night whispering
"beware". It was a set-up, Tash. Aunt Dina
told me Celeste makes most of her money
from people paying her for séances. She's an
old-fashioned fake. That's all.'

Tash frowned stubbornly. 'Fine. But that still
doesn't explain the lights and digging noise we
heard in the graveyard. Or my grandfather's
ghost detector working in the tree house *and*
at the crypt. Or the noises I heard in the house
last night. What about them? Are you saying
all that was Celeste too?'

'Something weird is going on, that's for
sure.' Sierra grinned, back to her old self now
she had a different problem to think about.

'Where did you hear the spooky noises, Tash?'

'I tracked them down to the library. They were loudest in there, but when I went in I couldn't see anything. That's when Mojo went a bit crazy barking and Mum chased me back to bed. I guess I got a bit of sleep, because the next thing I knew, it was morning. And I sent Mojo after you.'

The border terrier thumped the floor with his tail at the mention of his name. 'Good dog.' Tash leant down and gave him a pat.

'Let's search the library,' Elly said. 'I keep thinking Celeste is mixed up with these spooky lights and noises somehow. It's just her sort of thing. But how could she pull that stuff in your library? And why?'

'No reason I can think of,' Tash said. 'The only thing that makes sense is that my grandfather's ghost is haunting us.'

'Not that again,' groaned Sierra.

They argued about the existence of ghosts all the way to the library. Elly loved this room. It was dim and cool even on the hottest days. One wall held five long windows, with gauzy curtains drawn against the morning sun. The three other walls were lined with books from floor to ceiling. Leather chairs and sofas filled the space. The whole room smelt of leather and the lavender furniture polish made on the island and sold to tourists at extravagant prices.

'The noises were loudest on this side of the library.' Tash went to stand near the fireplace wall.

'There's nothing here but books,' Sierra said, standing with her hands on her hips.

Elly knelt and looked up the marble fireplace. It hadn't been used for months, and smelt faintly of tar and stale wood smoke, but she couldn't see anything except the inside of a chimney rising up and out of sight. 'Nothing in here.'

She jumped to her feet and saw Sierra wandering along the bookshelves, which were old dark wood, and built right into the wall. She was pressing on random bits of shelving. She reached the end and sighed.

'What are you doing?' Tash asked, her voice exasperated.

'Looking for the secret passage,' Sierra calmly explained, as she batted away the dust and pulled a few books from the shelf. 'Yuck! Nothing here but spiders. Eeuuw! Dead ones!'

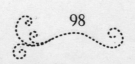

'Sierra's right. The noises had to come from somewhere,' Elly said. She knelt and emptied a row of books, pulling them off the shelf and stacking them on their sides. 'And there

wasn't anyone in
the room with
you so there has to
be some sort of tunnel
or room back here somewhere.'

'Not if it was a ghost.' But Tash shrugged and cleared another shelf of books. 'I suppose we can tell my mum we're spring cleaning,' she muttered, as a fresh cloud of dust rose. 'I better go and get the Hoover.'

'Wait!' Sierra shrieked. 'I've found something. Look!'

Elly jumped to her feet, dropping an armload of books with a crash. She and Tash crowded beside Sierra, peering into the dimly lit back of the shelf. There was some sort of tiny cupboard there, built into the wall. Elly could see it clearly: a small wooden door with a simple latch.

'That's no secret passage,' Tash snorted. 'Unless you're a mouse!'

Tash cleared the shelf of books. Sierra

reached in and lifted the latch. The door sprang open with a loud squeak of unoiled hinges. Elly felt her stomach muscles go tight with nerves. Sierra put her hand into the opening and pulled out something. It was a small, age-yellowed envelope. She stared at it for a moment, then handed it to Tash.

'It's your house,' Sierra said. 'You'd better open it.'

Tash stared down at the envelope in her hands, looking a bit scared. 'It won't be anything.' But she didn't sound as though she believed it.

'Well, you won't know that till you open it.' Elly felt she was going to burst with curiosity. 'Come on, I'm dying here.'

 'It isn't sealed.' Tash lifted the flap of the envelope. 'So I guess it's OK to…' She slid out a piece of folded cream-

coloured paper. Tash unfolded the paper gingerly. She stared at what was written on the paper for several seconds. Then she gasped. 'My grandfather wrote this! I recognize his handwriting.'

'What does it say?' For a moment Elly allowed herself to believe in Old Man Blake's ghost. What if he'd been haunting them because of this message? Had he wanted them to find it?

'It doesn't say anything.' Tash held the paper out for them to see.

Elly stared over her shoulder and saw that someone had written groups of capital letters on the paper, long strings and shorter strings of letters—but none of them made words. Had Tash's grandfather been mad after all? She glanced up at her friend, worried that this paper would upset her even more. But instead, Tash was looking determined.

'It means something,' Tash said. 'My grandfather is sending us a message. We just need to figure it out.'

'Actually, Tash,' Sierra's voice was suddenly thoughtful. She was frowning at the paper intently. 'I think you're right. I think this is a message. A message written in code!'

Chapter 10

'My brain hurts!' Tash glared at the computer screen. 'Replacement codes, binary codes, book codes, keyword codes…Why does it have to be so complicated?'

'Um…because the whole purpose of a code is to stop people figuring it out?' Sierra said. They were in Tash's bedroom, using her computer. Sierra sat at the keyboard, her fingers clicking away as she pasted the message into one code-breaking program after another. 'But all codes can be broken. There's bound to be something on here that will work, eventually.'

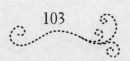

Elly yawned. Staying up late last night was making her sleepy. And trying to break a code was a lot harder in real life than it sounded. It had been fun at first but it was taking way too long. Sierra and Tash didn't seem to notice. They were glued to the computer screen.

Elly sighed and flopped onto her back on the floor. When the doorbell rang downstairs, she rolled over and jumped to her feet. 'I'll get it!' she called as she ran for the door. Sierra didn't answer. Tash merely grunted.

Elly clattered down the stairs but slid to a stop when she saw Tash's butler, Jasper, opening the door. Beaten to it! Elly turned and started to creep back upstairs when a familiar voice made her stop and turn back towards the door. Jasper had let in two visitors. One was Professor Partlow, which wasn't surprising.

But…Elly's eyes widened in shock. Standing next to him was Russell, the boy who had nearly shut them in the crypt!

'My nephew.' Professor Partlow's high-pitched voice was unmistakable. 'He will, of course, not be allowed to touch any of the inventions. Now, could you take me to where the machines are stored?'

'If you wouldn't mind just waiting here in the hall for a moment,' Jasper said. 'I'm afraid Mrs Blake-Reynolds wasn't expecting you this morning. She's working, but I'll see if she can spare you a few moments.' Jasper whisked out of sight.

Elly remained where she was, frowning down at the professor and his companion. Russell was Professor Partlow's nephew. It was hard to believe: Russell seemed a nice normal sort of boy, but she supposed he couldn't help it if the professor was his uncle. And why had

Russell run away the moment he saw his uncle in town?

She noticed that Professor Partlow was watching Jasper walk away. When Jasper was out of sight, the professor twitched his long nose right and left, like a rat sniffing for cheese. 'In here, quick!' Professor Partlow grabbed Russell by the back of his T-shirt and propelled him into the sitting room. Elly's last glimpse of them was the look of wide-eyed surprise on Russell's face as he was shoved through the door.

What was Professor Partlow up to? Elly slipped down the stairs, her flip-flops totally silent. Good sneaking-around shoes, she thought, grinning to herself, even though she was feeling slightly scared at spying on a grown-up. But she didn't trust Professor

Partlow. He was acting too weirdly.

She crept up to the sitting room door. The professor had left it slightly ajar, and Elly put her ear to the crack.

'Where is the dratted thing? You're in the way, boy, go and stand over by the window.'

I'm going to find out what he's after, Elly thought. She eased the door open. Jasper kept the hinges oiled and it opened silently. She stood in the doorway, watching Professor Partlow. He looked like a strange long-legged brown bird in his dusty tweed suit as he prowled round and round the display cases in the middle of the room. They contained the few of Old Man Blake's inventions that had actually worked, once.

'Where can the blasted thing be?' Professor Partlow bent over, his nose pressed against a case.

'Where's what?' Elly stepped into the room, doing her best to sound calm.

'Where did you come from?' The professor whirled round, his face growing bright red.

'I'm visiting Tash,' Elly explained politely. 'Are you looking for something?'

'No!' Partlow blinked and cleared his throat. 'I'm just wondering where the interesting artefacts are. If this is the best of the lot...' He looked around the room and sniffed in disdain, '...I'm wasting my time coming all the way to Sunday Island.'

'Well, I hope you're having a nice holiday anyway. Hi, Russell.' She turned to the boy, who was standing in the window looking, she noticed, terrified to see her.

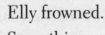

Elly frowned.

Something strange was definitely going on. But before she could ask another question, the door

sprang open and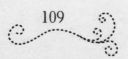
Tash's mum strode
into the room.

'Professor Partlow,
how nice to see you again.
I'm free if you want to discuss my father's
inventions now.'

Professor Partlow tugged at his jacket with
twitchy fingers and smiled broadly. 'Gracious
of you, Mrs Blake-Reynolds. My apologies
for bursting in here, but I couldn't control
my curiosity.'

'But you said—' Elly began.

'It would be very helpful,' Professor Partlow
interrupted, 'if you entertained Russell while
Mrs Blake-Reynolds and I discuss grown-up
matters. Perhaps you could all go outside to
play,' he added pointedly.

Elly stared at him. Go outside to play? Did
he think they were *six*?

Tash's mum turned to Elly with a
sympathetic smile. 'It would be very kind,

Elly. I'd appreciate it if you girls could look after Professor Partlow's nephew. We are going to be a tediously long time, I fear.'

'That's fine, Mrs Blake-Reynolds. Come on, let's go and find Tash and Sierra.'

Russell scampered after her. 'I-I hope you don't mind my uncle,' he stammered. 'I never actually met him before this holiday. He's my mum's half-brother and he never comes to visit because he's always working. He's quite a famous historian, actually.' He stamped up the stairs beside her. 'He acts funny sometimes because he's not used to kids. That's what my mum says. He's all right, really…' He sounded uncertain.

Elly tried to think of something nice she could say about the professor. She was still thinking as she opened the door to Tash's bedroom. She

pushed the door
wide open and
stood back to let
Russell enter. He took
one step into the room
and burst out laughing.

'Nice try!' he said between giggles. 'But I
can see your flip-flops!'

Elly pushed in behind Russell and found
herself facing a pair of tall white ghosts
wearing flip-flops: one pair pink; one purple.
'OK, guys,' Elly sighed. 'Why have you got
sheets over your heads?'

'Didn't we scare you?' Sierra's voice floated
mournfully out beneath the bed sheet,
sounding muffled and sad. 'Just a little?'

'No.' Elly shook her head, then realized they
couldn't see her. They hadn't cut eye holes.

'Amateur effort,' Russell said. 'Sheets look
like sheets. You could try covering your
clothes with flour and using white make-
up. But the ghost thing is pretty hard to pull

off. Ghosts just look like people, don't they? Maybe a bit see-through or something…'

'Russell, is that you?' Sierra tugged the sheet off her head. 'What are you doing here?'

'That's rude, Sierra.' Tash had pulled off her sheet too and was remaking her bed with sailor-like efficiency. When she finished she turned and smiled at Russell. 'But I want to know too. Why *are* you here?'

'His uncle is Professor Partlow,' Elly said. 'He's talking to your mum now.'

'Never mind,' Sierra said in a kind voice. 'You can't be held responsible for your relatives.'

'Sierra!' Tash glowered at her.

'It's OK.' Russell heaved a sigh. 'I don't like him much either. My parents thought I'd never get another chance to go to Sunday Island for a whole month. But I'd rather be back in Wilmslow with my friends. And besides…' his eyes sparkled, '…Uncle Peter may be a bit strange, but at least he doesn't go around dressing up in sheets and pretending to be a ghost. That was pretty lame.'

'Yeah. What was that about?' Elly shook her head in amazement.

'It's only…' Sierra paused for effect. Tash watched impassively, her sparkling eyes giving away her excitement. 'That Natasha Blake-Reynolds and Sierra Cruz are world-class geniuses.'

'Since when is wearing a sheet over your head a sign of super-intelligence?' Elly nudged Russell, who grinned.

Sierra leapt and pirouetted across the room, her pink flip-flops skimming over the carpet. 'We were practising. We're going to do a ghost tour of Sunday Island. What do you think of that? Genius, or what?'

'Uh…why would you want to do a ghost tour?' Russell stared at Elly's friends blankly.

Elly shut her mouth, which had somehow dropped open. 'Yeah? Why?'

'Investigations, my dear Watson,' Sierra said.

'It's the perfect way to research Sunday Island's ghosts,' Tash added. 'You know, things that go bump in the night? We can ask lots of questions about sightings and myths and legends, and no one will get suspicious because they'll think we're setting up the ghost tour.'

'Clever…' Elly still didn't believe in ghosts, but there was something spooky going on, and she wanted to find out what it was. Particularly now that someone…or something…was targeting Tash's house.

'My dad can write a script for the tour,' Sierra said. 'And Elly, you're going to be the star, of course. You

will be the tour
leader and do the
dramatic readings.
It's just like acting.
You'll be perfect.'

'And we'll make enough money so that
Sierra's dad won't have to sell up and leave
Sunday Island,' Tash added.

'You *are* geniuses,' Elly said. 'Count me in.'

'I don't think the money idea's so great.'
Sierra's smile faded. 'Dad and I can't just take
the tour money. I mean, my dad will think it's
charity and…'

'Don't worry,' Elly said. 'You'll earn it. A
production like this will be a huge amount of
work, so let's get started. Hey, Russell, would
you like to help with the tour?'

'Wow, can I?' He had fallen silent during
the discussion about ghosts, but now his
face brightened. 'I'm pretty good at drawing.
Would you like me to design a flyer? And I
can put them through all the doors and hand

them out to tourists. And we should make a sandwich board: you know, like giant cards you wear on your front and back. I'll walk around town with it, so everyone knows about the tour.'

'That is a brilliant idea.' Tash grabbed some pencils and paper from her desk. 'Start designing! We'll sort out the tour route.' She ran to her computer and opened a new tab. 'The forecast is good for tomorrow night: no rain and not much wind. And the moon's nearly full so people won't stumble over headstones or fall into my grandad's grave.'

Russell had started drawing a picture of a trio of ghosts on his paper. Now his head jerked up. 'Gravestones? You aren't going to go to the graveyard, are you?'

'Well, it's sort of an obvious place to go.' Elly watched Russell's eyes grow

round and the smile
slip from his face.
What was wrong?

'Actually, I don't think
messing around with ghosts is
a good idea.' Russell got slowly to his feet.

'What?' Tash stared at him in amazement.
'You were all for it a moment ago. Are you
scared, or something? You don't have to
come, you know. To the graveyard, I mean.'

'Of course I'm not scared.' Russell's face
had gone pink. Elly felt suddenly sorry
for him. He looked desperate. But what
was wrong?

'Russell? Time to go!' Professor Partlow's
voice floated up the stairs.

'Uhh…' Russell hesitated. His face grew
pinker. 'Look. Better count me out. But, it's
been nice…uh.' His voice trailed off. He
stared at them, looking miserable. 'See you.
Bye, Mojo.' He gave the dog a last pat on the
head then ran from the room.

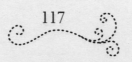

'Wow.' Sierra's voice broke the silence. 'I wonder what that was all about?'

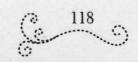

Chapter 11

'What if no one shows?' Sierra's voice rang out across the darkening town square. It was twilight and, except for them, the square was practically empty. Elly knew she ought to be worried, but mostly she wanted to giggle. Tash and Sierra looked so funny. They wore sheets with holes cut in for head and arms, and had painted their faces with white make-up, drawing big blue circles around their eyes. Even Mojo was in costume. Aunt Dina had drawn a dog's skeleton in luminous paint on one of the border terrier's winter overcoats.

Elly smoothed down her velvet jacket

and adjusted her three-cornered hat. Aunt Dina had made her a sort of town crier's costume since she was to be the tour guide. Elly's stomach squiggled with nerves and excitement. If anyone does show up, she thought, I just hope I don't forget my lines!

'I have a premonition,' Celeste said. 'Tonight will be very successful. Trust me.' She wore black, as usual, so all Elly could see of her was her face, floating above the ground like a doughy bun with two large currants for eyes.

'It's a bit early still. I'm sure the tourists will come.' Aunt Dina smiled encouragingly through her vampire make-up. 'It's quite an adventure. Sunday Island's first Ghost Tour!'

'I handed out dozens of leaflets,' Celeste added.

Elly tried to be grateful. She didn't point out that Celeste had also handed out leaflets about her website at the same time, drumming up business. Or that she had insisted on coming with them and then butted in all the time when the girls were gathering ghost stories from long-term island residents. That had been annoying, but Celeste had worked hard to help make the tour happen. And she did seem to know a lot about ghosts. Elly had been impressed in spite of herself.

Elly didn't know what to think about Celeste, but she still couldn't trust her aunt's friend. She hadn't imagined the fishing line and curtain. Or the smartphone recording. Celeste was a fake. Elly had tried to tell Aunt Dina several times about what she had found out the night of the séance. But it never seemed the right moment. Plus, Elly didn't have any real proof. The wire would be long gone. And Celeste had thought up the perfect explanation for the recording.

'Here they come!' Tash jumped up and down with excitement and shook a chain she'd brought as a prop. It made a deliciously spooky rattle. Sierra joined in, wailing and uttering low blood-curdling moans. A handful of tourists, families with adults and children, were meandering across the square towards them. More people were appearing in the distance. Their audience had arrived.

The squiggles in Elly's tummy leapt into action again. Everyone was staring at her. Her mouth went dry and for a moment she couldn't swallow. Sierra gave her a little push and Elly stepped forward. 'Welcome, ghost hunters! You are very brave... or *very* foolish!'

She did her best evil laugh, and several audience members tittered nervously. 'Welcome to the Sunday Island Ghost Tour!' Elly dared a look at people's faces. Grown-ups and children alike were waiting for her next words, eyes wide with anticipation. Her stomach unclenched. This was fun!

Elly took a deep breath and continued: 'Prepare yourselves! We will be exploring the spookiest spots on the island. Scenes of ghost sightings. Places where the veil between this world and the next is torn! You will hear stories of love and loss, tragic death, excitement, mystery and terror as we explore the island's ghostly myths and legends! Now, does everyone have a torch?'

It felt very odd to be tramping out of town on the east road at night, at the head of an excited crowd. Strands of light from all the torches strayed through the darkness; laughter and random comments rose above the general mutter. Elly watched the not-quite-full moon rise, a squashed orange shape. The sky glowed with a mysterious silver light and Elly shivered with enjoyment and excitement. Tonight felt like a dream. Anything could happen!

Aunt Dina and Celeste were chatting with the grown-ups; Tash, Sierra, and Mojo minding the stragglers. The road sloped gently down beside the beach to their first stop, the old dried-up well just outside town, said to be haunted by a woman in a long white cloak.

Elly told the story and led them on to the next spooky spot: the bramble-covered remains of an ancient stone house on the road out of town. By the time they were halfway through the tour, the group of twenty tourists and their tour guides were firm friends. Parents and children alike seemed to enjoy

the old ghost stories of
the island and Elly's
retellings. Sierra's dad
had done a great job with
the script, and Sierra and Tash
made perfect ghost tour guides, rattling their
chains and wailing with almost no giggles.
Aunt Dina was a regal vampire and got in a
long chat with one of the mums who was an
artist from the mainland.

The only problem was Celeste, who
insisted on handing every tourist a leaflet
for her website and kept interrupting Elly
to talk about her experiences finding and
talking to ghosts. She was using their tour to
show off her own business! Celeste ruined
the story about the barn fire; the ancient
Neolithic settlement of tiny stone houses; the
old, abandoned chapel on the far end of the
island. By the time they got to the graveyard,
and the grand finale, Elly was fuming.

This bit was really going to be good, and

she didn't want Celeste spoiling it. Tash had rigged up some special effects in the Blake family crypt. She'd been working on it all day, and wouldn't tell Sierra or Elly anything about it except that it would be brilliant. She and Jasper had even cut down most of the brambles, so it was easy for the ghost tour to get to the crypt.

As they reached the crypt, Elly looked around. Yes, Tash and Mojo had disappeared. Tash was getting ready to spring her surprise on the tour. 'Gather round, everyone!' As Elly waited for the stragglers, Celeste wafted up.

'Can I talk to you for a minute?' Elly motioned Celeste to move out of earshot of the gathering crowd. 'Look, Celeste,' she whispered. 'Please don't interrupt me during this part. We've got something really special planned.

Promise?'

But Celeste didn't seem to be listening. She was gazing past Elly, a strange faraway look in her eyes. 'I sense a ghostly presence, here, in the graveyard,' she intoned.

Elly groaned. She should have known! 'Just drop it, OK?' she snapped.

Celeste's eyes popped back into focus. 'What do you mean?'

'I found the wire in the curtain after your so-called séance.' Elly lowered her voice. She didn't want Aunt Dina or anyone else to find out about Celeste this way. 'And the voice recording, don't forget. I don't believe you can talk to ghosts at all.'

Celeste opened her mouth, then shut it and stomped away. Elly nearly called after her to apologize. She shouldn't have said that. But the last stragglers had joined the main group. Her audience was waiting and

Celeste had disappeared. Elly tugged her velvet jacket straight and took her place in front of the tomb.

'Welcome, foolhardy souls, to the ancient and forbidding crypt of the Blake family. Known to be haunted by the ghost of Old Man Blake himself!' Elly paused for effect, and her audience murmured appreciatively. Tash had insisted on putting in the bit about her grandad.

Elly felt the tingle of anticipation run up and down her arms. The crypt was pretty scary even in daytime. Now it was almost midnight, and she didn't fancy going in the crypt that much herself—even for their own ghost tour. Oh well…no chickening out now.

The tourists were flicking their torches all over the entrance to the crypt as Elly and

Sierra opened the door. It made a ghastly creaking sound as they pulled it wider.

'Yikes!' Sierra squealed. 'I mean…Whoooo! Enter who dares!' She shook her chain menacingly, then jumped aside to let the tourists stream in. 'I'll come last,' she called to Elly. 'Just to make sure everyone's inside!'

'Thanks!' Elly took a deep breath and led the way into the crypt. The angel loomed in the harsh light of dozens of torches, a grey-winged creature. The tourists shrieked and laughed with delight. 'Now that's proper scary!' shouted one of the dads.

Elly felt the hairs on her arms prickle as she turned her back on the stone angel. She watched the last of the tourists crowd into the crypt, squashing together to let the last ones come down the stone steps. When everyone was inside there was hardly room to move.

Dozens of faces, brightly lit, stared at her,

full of anticipation. They wanted something good now. Elly saw Aunt Dina, standing tall and regal, and her aunt nodded at her. She knew Elly was scared. Please, Tash, don't let us down, Elly thought. And now I need to do my part.

'OK,' she called. 'Before we can begin I need all those torches turned off, please!'

Cries of mock dismay and laughter as the torches flicked out one by one. The crypt filled with a heavy, thick darkness. The tourists stopped laughing and talking and an uneasy silence fell. Feet scuffed on the stone floor. Someone coughed. Tension filled the darkness until Elly couldn't bear it any longer. She flicked on her torch and held it beneath her chin.

'You stand before the last resting place of the Blake family,' she said in her spookiest voice, and there was an outburst of relieved laughter from the invisible crowd. 'Generations lie here, bones of Blakes, mouldering, the souls long since departed and at rest. But...' Elly deepened her voice. It echoed eerily around the crypt, bouncing back to her from the ceiling.

'One Blake refuses to rest. His grave lies empty on the hillside above. The ashes of his body are scattered over the island, but the ghost of Old Man Blake is said to haunt this very crypt!'

Elly paused.

This was it. Her next lines were Tash's cue to set off the special effects. 'What can he want? Has he left a task undone in life? Is he trying to get a message to his descendants? When will he appear next? Perhaps, this very night!'

The echoes of her voice softened and

died. Elly waited. *Come on, Tash! That was your cue!* Still nothing. The crowd shuffled, shifted, sensing something had gone wrong. There was only one thing for it. Elly would have to improvise.

'Old Man Blake was known for his reclusiveness,' she invented. 'Perhaps there are too many of us here tonight for him to show himself. We had best depart as quietly and respectfully as we came, before the spirits take offence. Ladies and gentlemen, if you would—'

But before Elly could finish her sentence, a gust of cold wind surged through the crypt, smelling of damp earth and sea air, sending hats flying and Sierra's sheet fluttering madly.

'Ooooh!' The tourists murmured.

Then someone screamed.

Chapter 12

'Look!' shouted a woman. 'Beside the stone angel!'

Elly whirled round. There, standing in front of the angel, was a glowing white figure of an old man, tall and gaunt. Elly could see the angel right through it. How had Tash done it? Had she rigged up a projector or something? It was amazing!

Even though she knew Tash had made the ghostly apparition, Elly felt her heart kick into high gear. Her mouth dried and she swallowed hard. The figure stood, its faint outline dressed in old-fashioned clothes unruffled by the

133

wind still howling through the crypt. Slowly it lifted an arm and pointed to the darkness behind the stone angel. The wind rose to a shriek that hurt Elly's ears. As she raised her hands to cover them, the figure faded slowly, until at last it had completely vanished.

The wind died down. Elly lowered her hands, staring in blank amazement at the spot where Tash's ghost had appeared. Wow! That had been beyond anything she could have expected. Tash had ended the tour with true style.

As Elly slowly turned to face her audience, the tourists burst into spontaneous applause.

'How did you do that?'

'Brilliant!'

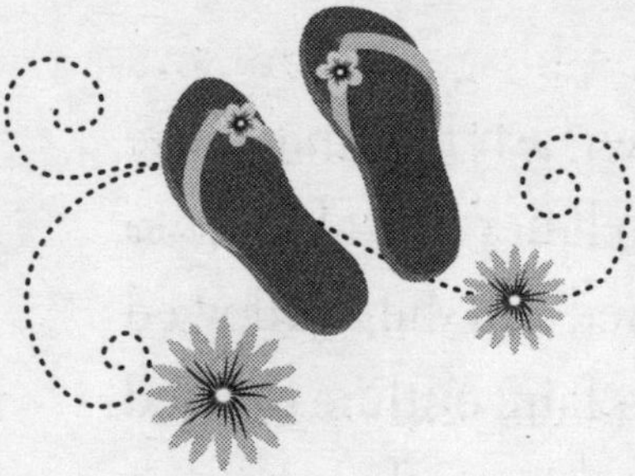

'Do it again! Mum, ask them to do it again!'

'Ladies and gentlemen.' Elly's heart was gradually returning to normal.

'Our tour is at an end. I hope you have enjoyed yourselves. My ghostly colleague will show you out of the crypt, and our lady vampire will be your guide back to town.' Elly waved at Sierra, who nodded, dodged out of the crypt and held the door for the tourists as they streamed past.

Elly got a lot of compliments for her acting, and she spotted many of the happy ghost hunters pressing tips into Sierra's hand as they filed out of the crypt. The last tourist melted into the night, following Aunt Dina, who was leading the march home. Celeste seemed to have vanished. Elly felt a bit guilty, but she was more curious as to where Tash had gone.

'Where's Tash?' Sierra propped the door open with a large stone. She draped her chain around her shoulders like a ghostly lord mayor, turned on her torch and joined

Elly in the crypt. 'I can't believe those special effects. I nearly wet myself. And how did she run the projector? Batteries? And that wind machine!'

'Maybe it was one of her grandad's inventions,' Elly said. She was getting worried now. Surely Tash should have come out by now to be told how amazingly clever she was. And where was Mojo? 'I think we should go and find her.'

'I was afraid you were going to say that.' Sierra sighed. 'Maybe she's just gone ahead to the tree house for our sleepover tonight?'

Elly shook her head. The crypt seemed spookier than ever now that they were alone. 'Tash?' Elly's voice bounced off the walls, hesitant and quavery. No answer. 'I don't like this.' Sierra's hand grabbed hold of the back of Elly's jacket. 'Where is she? ... *Tash!* Stop fooling around.'

'She's not here.' Elly shone her torch a second time around the crypt. It was empty of everything but the tomb itself, the angel, and a load of dust and cobwebs. There was only one place left Tash could be...

Elly moved forward, keeping the angel pinned in torchlight. She edged past it, not wanting to touch the stone. She shone her torch into the dark space between it and the wall.

Sierra peeked over her shoulder. 'A hole!' Her gasp rang round the crypt. Their torches revealed an opening in the wall a metre and a half high. Rubble was neatly piled beside it, together with a shovel. 'Someone's been digging here recently,' Sierra said, nudging the shovel with the toe of her flip-flops. 'Do you think Tash did that? Kinda creepy digging in a crypt.'

'Tash's ghost *was* pointing this way. She must want us to follow her,' Elly said. 'Just like the treasure hunt where we had to find her tree house. She really likes her games. Fine. I'll go if you will.'

'I guess…' Sierra whined.

Elly bent down and stepped through the hole.

She was in a dark passageway stretching out on either side of her—probably one of Sunday Island's famous World War Two tunnels. It was partly brick-lined, and had stout wooden beams every few metres, supporting the roof.

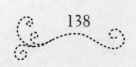

It looked as if it had been used recently too. A path had been trodden through the dusty floor, going left. More than one pair of feet had gone this way—and recently. Elly's

stomach squirmed.
Whoever was using
this tunnel, it wasn't
just Tash.

'Come on.' She headed
off, following the footprints. Sierra
moaned, but followed, keeping close behind.

The tunnel gently curved to the left, then
the right, then straightened out and headed,
it seemed to Elly, slightly uphill. In several
places it narrowed to get round granite
outcrops, and once they had to crawl on
hands and knees.

'I really, really don't like this,' Sierra
muttered over and over. 'I *am* claustrophobic,
you know.'

'There are air vents. Feel the breeze?'
Elly asked. 'This is really well engineered.
And Tash wouldn't send us somewhere
dangerous. She may like adventures and
mysteries, but underneath she's just as
sensible as her mother.'

'I know.' Sierra sighed as they got to their feet and shone their torches along the tunnel. 'I just don't like being underground. Five more minutes, then I'm going back.'

'OK.' Elly felt they'd gone long enough too. It was only ten minutes, but it felt a lot longer underground.

The ground began to rise under their feet, and round the next bend Elly's light shone on a short flight of stone steps leading up to a wooden door in a brick wall. A pile of old boards lay stacked beside the door, long rusting nails protruding along their lengths. Next to them was a crowbar.

'We're here.' Elly found she was whispering.

'Yeah,' Sierra said. 'But where is "here"?'

'Only one way to find out.' Elly climbed the steps.

'Wait!' Sierra grabbed her arm. 'That door

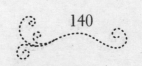

was boarded up.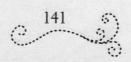
Someone's prised off
the boarding. Tash
didn't do that. And she
didn't dig through the crypt
into the tunnel either.'

'Sierra!' Elly felt her brain click as she realized what it meant. 'There aren't any ghosts. You were right. The noise we heard the other night in the graveyard was someone digging that hole into this tunnel. And these boards were prised off recently. The splinters are fresh.'

'I should be less scared,' Sierra said. 'But I'm not. What's going on? Who would do this? And why?'

'I don't know.' Elly examined the door. There didn't seem to be a doorknob, so she put out a hand and gave the door a gentle push. Nothing. She pushed harder and felt it give slightly. 'Give me a hand, Sierra. I think it's stuck.'

'But we don't know what we're walking into! This isn't one of Tash's jokes after all, remember?'

'I know. But we have to find her. She could be on the other side of that door, needing help.'

Sierra groaned. 'I guess you're right. Budge over.'

Elly squeezed over so Sierra could join her on the top step. They put their palms flat on the door and shoved. It resisted for a moment, then suddenly slid forward a few inches with a mournful, rusty squeal.

'Wait here till I give the OK,' Elly whispered to Sierra. She pushed her way through the gap, stood up and blinked as her eyes adjusted to moonlight streaming through a row of long windows. Hey, she was in—

Something hurtled into her legs and she

collapsed sideways
onto the ground.
No, not something.
Someone…

Winded, Elly struggled
to roll away, but her attacker was pinning her
down, clambering on top of her. She tried
to shout to Sierra to run for help, but all she
could manage was 'Oooff!'

A torch flicked on, and white light glared
into Elly's eyes, blinding her.

'Oh!' said a voice, sounding both disappointed
and relieved. 'It's you!'

'Tash?' Sierra was standing over them, her
torch flickering from Elly to her attacker and
back, her voice puzzled. 'Why are you sitting
on Elly?'

Chapter 13

'I spotted the tunnel when I was setting up my special effects for the ghost tour,' Tash said and propped open the door to the secret passageway with a heavy book. The tunnel started at the Blake family crypt and ended at the Sunday House library. Elly, Sierra, Tash, and Mojo huddled together.

'I followed the footprints in the tunnel and they led me right back here,' Tash whispered, 'but as soon as I came through, the bookcase swung shut behind me. It's on some sort of spring. I've been trying to figure out how to open it from inside the library ever since.

Then I heard you guys in the tunnel. I thought it was whoever's been trying to break into Sunday House. It's a miracle we didn't wake my mum. I want to figure out what's going on before we tell her.'

'Do you think it's burglars?' Sierra looked nervously into the tunnel.

'I suppose it could be...if they like dusty paintings or old books. There's a silver tea service somewhere.' Tash looked doubtful. 'But there are much better places on the mainland to rob. We don't even have a widescreen TV.'

'Maybe it's Celeste,' Elly blurted, then felt her face flush red as Sierra and Tash turned to stare at her.

'Why would Celeste...' Tash began. 'Oh...you think she's after Grandad's ghost detector?'

'She did seem really

interested in it at the séance.'

Sierra shook her head. 'I don't know who's been trying to break in. But one thing's clear at least. It isn't ghosts. Your house isn't haunted after all, Tash.'

Mojo trotted to the library door. Then he began to growl. It was a low and menacing sound that made the hair stand up on the back of Elly's neck.

Sierra gasped. 'There's someone out there,' she whispered. 'Maybe it's your mum or Jasper, Tash,' Elly said hopefully. 'Mojo wouldn't growl at them,' Tash replied. 'The burglar must have come through the tunnel before Tash!' Sierra's voice was shaking with panic. 'Everyone on the island knew we were doing our ghost tour. It would be the perfect time to break in. Oh my godfathers, the burglar must have been in the house this whole time.'

Tash's head jerked round to stare at Sierra, her eyes wide with dawning horror.

They all heard it: footsteps. Padding down the hall towards the library.

Elly leapt for the light switch and clicked it off. Tash grabbed Mojo and shushed him furiously. He whimpered but fell silent.

'What do we do?' Sierra's voice was breathless. Her torchlight shook. 'Shall we call your mum and Jasper? Or just barricade the library door with a sofa so they can't get in?'

'There isn't time!' Elly was listening, her ear to the door. 'They're here!' she hissed. 'Hide!' Tash crouched behind a chair; Elly and Sierra behind a sofa.

'We need to get help!' Sierra hissed.

'Shhhh!' Elly warned. There was the soft click of someone turning a doorknob. Tash put a hand over Mojo's muzzle, stifling his growl. Elly's heart was pounding. They were about to find out who was behind the lights in the graveyard; who had tunnelled from the crypt to Tash's house.

A triangle of light spread across the carpet as the library door slowly opened. Elly could just make out a tallish figure holding a small torch. And then Mojo wriggled free of Tash and began to bark furiously. The torch snapped out.

'Mojo! No!' Tash shouted. She lunged after the dog.

Elly jumped to her feet and darted forward, not sure what she was going to do except help Tash. Sierra was screaming at the top of her lungs and Elly realized she was yelling too. A figure stumbled past, swearing at the dog snapping at its ankles. Tash grabbed Mojo's collar just as a loud squeal of unoiled hinges was followed by the noise of the bookcase entrance thudding shut.

The intruder had escaped.

Mojo was still yapping in rage as Elly ran to turn the lights on. As she stood blinking beside the door, her eyes adjusting to the sudden bright light, Tash's mum burst into the room.

'What on earth? I thought you girls were sleeping over in the tree house tonight. What are you up to?' She did not look at all happy at being woken up.

'Mum, someone broke into the house!'

'What?!'

'There's a secret passage from the crypt—'

Mrs Blake-Reynolds groaned. 'Now, I really have had enough. I know it's been an exciting night with the ghost tour, but really, girls! Intruders?

Secret tunnel? I grew up in the house, Tash. Don't you think I'd know if there was a secret passage into Sunday House?'

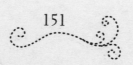

'I think you should look at this, Mrs Blake-Reynolds.' Sierra pointed to Mojo, who was sniffing and growling at something on the floor.

Tash's mum strode across the room for a closer look. Elly followed. It was a scrap of fabric. Brown tweed. Elly gasped.

'That's from Professor Partlow's suit,' Sierra said. 'I'd recognize that horrible fabric anywhere. Mojo must have torn it off his trousers. Professor Partlow dug a hole from your family crypt into one of the World War Two tunnels. The tunnel leads right to this room. I've walked through it, Mrs Blake-Reynolds, all the way from the crypt. And I hope I never have to do it again!' She shivered.

Mrs Blake-Reynolds picked up the fabric

and stared at it. 'I can't believe it. There must be some other explanation.' Her face was shocked. 'Professor Partlow is a reputed historian. Surely…' She looked at Tash, Elly, and Sierra in turn. 'You say you've all been through the tunnel.'

'Mum, I don't make things up. You know that.' Tash looked her mother in the eyes.

Mrs Blake-Reynolds nodded. 'I know, Natasha. So there's a tunnel leading to this room. I wonder why my father never told me.' Her voice sounded suddenly sad. 'It must have been built when he was here.'

She sighed. 'I don't want to believe it, but I fear we've nearly been the victim of a scam. The professor must have been trying to steal your grandfather's inventions. But as to why…' She shook her head. 'I'd better go and phone the constable and wake Jasper.'

Elly watched Tash's mother stride purposefully out of the room. Tash picked up Mojo and gave him a cuddle. 'Quiet now. You were right all along, clever dog!' She smiled at Elly and Sierra. 'He never liked Professor Partlow.'

'But he does like Russell!' Sierra added. 'Do you suppose the kid knows what his uncle is up to?'

'He must do.' Elly felt a bit sick. 'And he seemed so nice. I can hardly believe it. But he was snooping around the crypt, and he was with Professor Partlow here yesterday, helping search for whatever they're after.'

'And he didn't want us to include the graveyard on the ghost tour,' Tash added. 'Remember how he refused to help us after he found out we were going there tonight? He knows all right.'

'So the Mojo-ometer got it wrong!' Sierra

pointed at the border terrier. 'Is he one of your grandad's inventions too?'

'Ha. Ha.' Tash said flatly.

'Uhhh…wait a minute.' Elly's brain was ticking over fast, and everything added up to an emergency!

'What's up, Sherlock?' Sierra asked.

'Tash,' Elly said. 'Your mum said she thinks Professor Partlow is after one of your grandad's inventions.'

Tash nodded.

'And when he was here with Russell I overheard him complaining that "it" wasn't here,' Elly continued. 'So maybe he came back tonight to have another look round. But I'm pretty sure he wasn't carrying anything when he came into the library. Which means he didn't find what he was looking for…And

there's only one other place "it" could be.'

'The tree house!' Tash shouted.

'But…' Sierra shook her head. 'None of those pieces of junk work. You know they don't, Tash!'

'Maybe.' Tash put Mojo down. Her face was growing pink with determination. 'But Professor Partlow has risked a lot to steal one of them.'

'He doesn't know about the tree house,' Elly protested.

'But we can't wait for him to find out. And aren't you dying to know what he's looking for?' Without another word, Tash turned and ran out of the library, flip-flops slapping on the wooden floor. Mojo darted after her.

'Wait,' called Sierra. 'Shouldn't we tell your mum…?' But Tash was already gone. Sierra groaned and looked beseechingly at Elly.

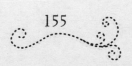

'Do we have to?'

'What do you think?' Elly sprinted after Tash.

Clouds covered the moon and the night was dark and oddly still. For once there wasn't a hint of breeze. As she ran through the night, it seemed to Elly as if the island was holding its breath.

She soon caught Tash up. They ran shoulder to shoulder, Sierra pattering at their heels. Mojo seemed to know where they were headed, and led the way. Even without moonlight lighting their path, Elly could make out his small shape bounding over the heather in front of them. They reached the maze in minutes, and Mojo disappeared inside. Elly started after him but Tash reached out and grabbed her arm, pulling her to a stop.

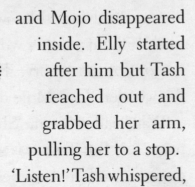

'Listen!' Tash whispered,

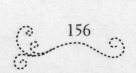

hugging Elly and Sierra close. 'I heard something.'

Elly heard it too, the pounding of feet down the hillside. She glanced back. She could hardly breathe. Someone was following them.

'Oh my godfathers!' Sierra cried. 'That's Professor Partlow, isn't it?'

Tash slumped into her two friends. 'We've led him right to the tree house and the rest of Grandad's inventions.'

'He doesn't know the way through the maze,' Elly said. 'We can beat him to the tree house.'

'And then do what?' Sierra demanded, her whisper outraged. 'We have to go back and tell your mum and Jasper. We can't cart off all those box-loads of inventions on our own.'

'Well, he's not just helping himself to them.'

Before Elly could stop her, Tash had darted into the maze. Sierra stamped her foot in frustration, but ran after her anyway. Elly followed.

Tash was on a mission. Elly didn't know what they could do to stop the professor if he was determined to steal Old Man Blake's inventions from the tree house, but she couldn't desert her friends. *Oh help!* she thought as she ran into the darkness of the maze. First ghosts, now burglars. She didn't know which was scarier.

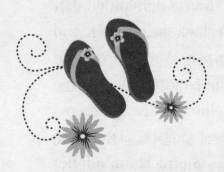

Chapter 14

Gasping with relief, Elly, Sierra, and Tash with Mojo under one arm clambered up the rope ladder to the tree house. As they burst through the door, Tash immediately started sorting through her grandfather's inventions. Mojo was scampering around, sniffing at every invention as if he was helping. Elly suddenly felt a wave of exhaustion sweep over her. It was nearly midnight.

'Pull up the rope ladder,' Tash instructed Sierra.

Sierra quickly obeyed, dumping the rope with its wooden bars on the platform outside

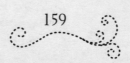

the tree house entrance. She shut the door behind her. 'Wish this had a lock,' she said. 'I can see a light at the edge of the maze. It'll take him time, but he'll find his way in… What're we gonna do when he gets here?'

Tash sat back on her heels and shook her head wearily. 'I don't get it. I mean, I love Grandad's inventions. But I've just been through everything here again, and there isn't anything that seems valuable. What is Professor Partlow after?' She jumped to her feet, grabbed a pen and paper off the table and began to write a note. 'I'll send Mojo to Mum with a message to get over here, then I'll climb onto the roof and try to get a phone signal. I think we need help.'

Tash finished writing the note and knelt beside Mojo, tucking the scrap of paper into the message carrier on his collar.

Tash gave him a pat. 'I need your help. Go find Mum. Find Mum! Good dog!' Tash carried Mojo outside to the platform and put him in the basket she used as a doggy lift. The basket was suspended over the side of the platform on a simple pulley. She gave Mojo a last kiss, then lowered him down. The rope fed through the squeaking wheels of the pulley until Mojo reached the ground. Elly watched him jump out of the basket and scamper off into the maze.

As Tash turned to go back into the tree house, Elly gasped and caught her arm, pointing in warning. The light flickered closer, moving slowly through the maze. If it was Professor Partlow, he was over halfway to the tree house!

A high-pitched male voice rose out of the distant shadows: 'Look! It's that little girl's dog.

Grab him, Russell!' There were scrabbling noises and shouting. Elly recognized Professor Partlow's voice.

Elly felt Tash's arm tense under her hand. 'It's OK,' she said quickly. 'No one can catch Mojo when he doesn't want them to.'

Tash nodded, watching the light, which had steadied and was moving forward again. 'I'm going on the roof now.' Her calm voice had an edge of anger beneath it Elly had never heard before. 'You and Sierra see if you can find some ammo. In case we have to repel boarders!' Using the window ledge as a ladder, Tash scrambled up onto the tree house roof.

Elly took a last look at the professor's torchlight. She could hear him and Russell crashing through the maze now. Russell seemed to be arguing with his uncle,

but Elly didn't stay
to hear what he was
saying. She darted
back into the tree house.

Sierra had obviously had the same idea
about ammunition, and was gathering
together a pile of books and cushions. She
looked up at Elly and shrugged. Her face was
pale with exhaustion.

'The trouble is,' Sierra said, 'cushions aren't
going to give him much of a headache. And
I refuse to sacrifice the packets of sweets. I'm
starving!' She grinned, but Elly could see she
was scared stiff.

'Let's get this stuff out onto the platform.'
Elly's own heart was beginning to thud
uncomfortably.

Elly and Sierra shifted their pile of ammo
out onto the platform as Professor Partlow's
torchlight twisted and turned through the
maze. It had nearly reached them! Elly could
hear Tash on the roof punching buttons on

her phone and mumbling about Sunday Island's rubbish telephone reception.

Finally, with a grunt of pure frustration, Tash slid off the roof, dangling from her arms for a second before dropping to land beside them with a thud. 'No luck,' she said, her voice tense. 'We're on our own.'

A tall figure in tweed pushed out of the hedge into the clearing around the tree house. It was Professor Partlow, and he was dragging Russell behind him. The professor blinked in surprise at the sight of the enormous tree rising out of the maze, cradling a small wooden tree house five metres in the air.

'You!' Partlow's eyes narrowed and he glared at Tash. 'You have your grandad's inventions up there, don't you?'

Tash arched an eyebrow and then nodded.

'You don't have a clue what you've got,' he shouted at her.

Tash picked up a book, handing another to Elly. Sierra grabbed a cushion. 'Go away!' Tash ordered. 'You're not stealing my grandfather's inventions. I won't let you! I've phoned the constable, and he's going to be here any minute. I'd run for it, if I were you.'

Professor Partlow gave a scratchy laugh. 'I don't believe you. Russell, climb the tree!' As he stepped forward, he must have loosened his grip on Russell's arm, because the boy twisted away.

'I won't help you!' he shouted. 'I like them! And I don't like you!' With that, Russell dodged back into the maze. Elly heard his footsteps pattering into the distance. Excellent! She'd been right about Russell: he was a nice kid after all.

Professor Partlow started after him, then whirled back round, the coat-tails of his tweed jacket flaring like a scarecrow's. He scowled up at them. 'I'll climb the tree myself.'

As he advanced on the tree house, Elly found herself stepping backwards. But there was nowhere to run. They were trapped.

Chapter 15

Professor Partlow reached up a long tweedy arm and grabbed a tree branch. 'Oof!' he grunted as he swung himself up. His pointed brown shoes scraped at the tree. He found a foothold and clung to the trunk like a giant brown cicada. 'Come on!' he shouted, puffing. His red face peered up at them. 'The invention is of no use to you.'

Tash leant over the edge of the platform. 'No.' She dropped the book she was holding and it fell with a flurry of flapping pages, clonking the professor on the nose.

'Ow!' Professor Partlow fell backwards out

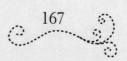

of the tree, arms and legs windmilling, and landed on the ground with a thud. Sierra's cushion fell onto his face, muffling his angry howl.

'Oooh!' she squealed.

Elly found she was shaking. The look on Partlow's face as he shoved himself to his feet scared her. She clutched her book tightly.

'Go away, Professor Partlow!' Tash shouted.

'I'm not going anywhere until I have that invention.' Professor Partlow was shaking with rage. 'And three silly little girls aren't going to stop me.'

'Silly yourself!' shouted Sierra. She was pointing at the entrance to the maze. 'Look behind you!'

'Don't be ridiculous,' the professor sneered. 'This isn't a pantomime.'

'And I'm not a pantomime policeman.'

A new voice boomed across the tree house clearing. 'Which is why I'm going to arrest you!'

Elly's heart leapt as Sunday Island's only policeman, Billy Matthews, strode into the clearing. Russell crept behind him, looking at once scared and triumphant.

'I told you to leave them alone,' Russell said to his uncle, who seemed suddenly to have shrunk to a much smaller man.

Professor Partlow stammered and stuttered at the sight of the stern-faced constable. Elly felt giddy with relief and grabbed onto the railing to keep from falling over. Sierra was whooping with delight. Tash dropped the book she was holding and lowered the rope ladder.

Elly followed Tash and Sierra down the ladder. As she jumped the last few feet to the ground, Mojo rushed into the clearing, barking and wagging his tail. She watched him fling himself at Tash, who scooped the dog into her arms.

Mrs Blake-Reynolds burst through the maze entrance after the border terrier. 'Natasha!' she cried. 'Thank heavens you're safe. Mojo brought me your message just as the constable was arriving. We got here as fast as we could.'

'Clever dog.' Tash giggled as Mojo licked the end of her nose.

'And this lad helped me through the maze,' said the constable, laying a hand on Russell's shoulder.

'If you'd caught that beast when I told you to…' Professor Partlow whirled on Russell, who shrank back.

Aunt Dina sprinted into the tree house clearing, her black cloud of curly hair bouncing with every step. She was still in pyjamas and a long red dressing gown and looked fierce enough to slay dragons. Celeste pattered after her, puffing and holding her side.

'Aunt Dina, what are you doing here?' Elly asked, rushing to her aunt for a hug.

'Tash's mum called me after she called the constable,' Aunt Dina started. 'I heard the noise —'

'I told you, Dee,' Celeste wheezed, her dark-ringed eyes wide with indignation. 'That man has a dark aura.'

Billy Matthews stepped forward. 'You're already under arrest, Professor Partlow. Don't make things worse for yourself. I think you'd best come along with me to the police station now.'

'This is all your fault, you silly boy,' Professor Partlow said, poking Russell, who was now close to tears, in the chest. 'Everything would have been fine if you'd just done as you were told.'

'Leave the poor boy alone!' Aunt Dina scooped Russell out of Professor Partlow's reach, raising herself to her full six feet and glaring at the professor. 'It's quite obvious that you have no business being in charge of a child.'

'But you can't arrest me.' Professor Partlow began to stutter. 'I-I'm a-an important historian. These girls are obstructing my research. If you arrest me, I will never tell you the secrets of Blake's invention and I…' His voice trailed away as the policeman took him by the arm and led him out of the maze.

Russell watched his uncle being taken away. His face was white and Elly noticed that he was shivering. He turned

to face her. 'I...I'm really sorry.' He looked imploringly from her to Tash and then Sierra. 'My uncle researched all the old tunnels on the island and realized that he could get into Sunday House by clearing one of them. I helped him dig from the crypt into the tunnel. He told me he was doing important history stuff. Said he was on to a big discovery. I didn't know he wanted to rob you. Then tonight he made me come with him.'

'What did he want to steal?' Tash asked. 'Mum would have probably sold him any of the inventions, maybe even given them to him. They don't really work after all.'

'He told me one of those inventions was really important and worth a lot of money. My uncle wanted all the credit for the invention and the money all to himself.' Russell wouldn't look at any of them now.

'Which one?' Elly asked. She could feel excitement bubbling in her tummy. Another mystery to solve.

'What does it do?' Sierra was bouncing. 'Why is it important? What is it worth?'

Russell just shrugged.

'But how did he know about the tree house?' Tash asked.

'We saw you running from Sunday House and he decided to follow you and you know the rest.' Russell's lip started to quiver. 'Don't let them arrest me. Please!'

'We won't let anyone arrest you,' Elly said. 'You were very brave to run away and help the police.'

Russell still looked uncertain.

'I guess you're a hero.' Sierra patted him on the back. 'And we still owe you an ice cream!'

Tash put a
squirming Mojo
on the ground,
and the dog ran to
Russell. The boy gathered
Mojo in his arms with a shaky sob. He buried
his face in Mojo's fur, and when he looked up
at last, his face was tear-stained. Elly felt her
own eyes burn. Poor kid.

Aunt Dina gave Russell a reassuring smile.
'You'll be fine, young man. But your parents
need to know what's been going on. They'll
want you home at once, I should imagine.'

Mrs Blake-Reynolds stepped forward and
held out her hand. 'I think you'd better come
home with me and phone your parents. You
can stay at Sunday House until they're able to
come for you. And I'm sure Jasper can rustle
up some bacon sandwiches for a late-night
dinner. What do you say, Russell?'

Russell nodded. 'I'd like that.'

Tash's mother smiled at him. 'And girls,

you come and have some sandwiches too. You must be starving. Dina, Celeste, will you join us?'

'I'd be delighted.' Aunt Dina turned to Elly. 'You girls have been very brave and very clever, but thank goodness this adventure is at an end.'

Elly looked at Sierra and Tash. 'Can we stay here a bit longer? There's something we have to do.'

'We'll be right along, Mum. As soon as we solve the mystery of Grandad's invention.'

'Hmmm.' Mrs Blake-Reynolds frowned. 'Very well. But be quick. And don't blame me if we eat all the bacon! Agreed, Dina?'

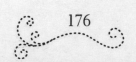

'I suppose.' Aunt Dina wrapped Elly in a big hug then turned to go. 'Don't be too long,' she said.

Tash climbed the tree

house ladder one-handed, carrying a sleepy Mojo.

'Oh, but there's bacon that way!' Sierra cried, pointing after Russell and Mrs Blake-Reynolds. 'I'm starving, Tash! Hang on.' She scampered up the ladder after her friend.

Elly was about to follow when she noticed Celeste trailing after the others out of the maze. 'Celeste, wait!'

Startled, Celeste turned back. 'What is it, Elly?'

'Look.' Elly bit the inside of her lip. This wasn't easy to say. 'About the wire in the curtain; about the voice recording. I don't care what you believe, but I don't want you to lie to people any more. I won't tell Aunt Dina if you promise never to rig your séances again. It's tricking people, and it's not right.'

Celeste sighed. 'The young are so certain they know best. The truth is, I *am* sensitive,

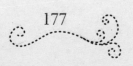

Elly. I do feel spirits. But…people want more than that. They want show business. Entertainment.' Her eyes glazed over for a moment, then she shook her head and looked at Elly. 'Very well. I promise. Friends?' She held out her hand.

Elly nodded. 'OK.' She shook Celeste's hand and watched the medium turn and follow after the others. Then she swung up the rope ladder to join Tash and Sierra.

Chapter 16

When Elly entered the tree house, the first thing she saw was Mojo, curled up asleep on top of the puzzle box. Tash and Sierra sat beside him, staring at it. Elly settled onto a floor cushion and reached out to touch the smooth wood with a finger.

'It's got to be this,' she said. 'Hasn't it?'

'It's the only thing that makes sense.' Tash frowned at the box. 'I couldn't think straight with Professor Partlow after us, but this was the one thing Grandad left me in his will. It must mean it's more valuable than all the others. So the question is, why? What's in there?'

'Gold!' Sierra gazed at the box in awe. 'I told you so. That's why the creepy Partlow wanted it. It's full of a fortune in solid gold.'

'I don't think so.' Elly shook her head. 'It's not really heavy enough. We're going to have to figure out how to open it. I vote we don't leave the tree house until we've solved the puzzle.'

'Me too.' Tash nodded.

'Bacon!' wailed Sierra. Tash gave her a stern look. 'Oh all right. But you need to move Mojo, Tash. We can't be geniuses with a dog sleeping all over the evidence.'

'Wake up, Mojo!' Tash reached into her pocket and pulled out a handful of dog treats.

'Come on, boy. Midnight feast!'

'That's not fair!' Sierra cried. 'He gets to eat while we starve.'

'You're welcome to some of these.' Tash held one up with

a grin. 'Mojo will share.'

'Very funny.' Sierra wrinkled her nose. 'Yuck!'

Mojo sat up on the puzzle box and Tash fed him a treat. He crunched it eagerly with sharp white teeth, then yawned. He stood up, each of his four paws on a corner of the box, stretched and shook himself, from his nose to the tip of his tail. Then he yelped in dismay and leapt off the box. The top half had clicked and slid partly open.

'Mojo!' Tash shrieked. 'Clever dog. You've done it!'

'Of course,' cried Elly. 'You must have to press on all four corners of the box at once. No wonder you never figured it out before, Tash. You'd need four hands to do that yourself. Or four paws.'

'Never mind all that.' Sierra was peering into the box. 'What's in there?'

Tash slid the lid fully open. Her hands were

 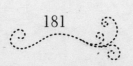

shaking. 'Wow.' Her voice sounded puzzled and awed at the same time. 'It…It's another of Grandad's inventions.' She reached inside the box, lifted out a machine and set it on the floor. Elly stared at it, trying to work out what it could be. It was square and metal, with lots of cogs and gears, and it reminded her more than anything of pictures of old typewriters she'd seen in books.

'Wait a minute. I think I know what this is!' Sierra leant forward to examine the invention, her eyes wide with excitement. 'Don't you remember when we were researching on the internet, Tash? We saw something sort of like this. This…' she paused for effect, '…is a code machine!'

'You mean it translates normal words into code?' Elly asked, staring at the machine in awe. 'That's the sort of thing spies used to use.'

'And the other way round. It should break the same code.' Tash gasped and Elly got it at the same moment.

'The letter in the library!' They all shouted at once.

'This machine should decode it,' Tash said. 'Mojo! You've done it!' She hugged the yawning border terrier. 'Grandad always did like treasure hunts and mysteries.' She grinned. 'I guess I take after him.'

'Let's go and get the coded message and figure it out now.' Elly jumped up and started to tug Sierra to her feet.

'Take it easy,' Sierra groaned. 'I'm weak from lack of food.'

'It's OK.' Tash scrambled up. 'Don't move.' She ran to one of her whale posters that covered the tree house walls, lifted the frame and felt behind it. 'I put it here for safe keeping.'

'You hid it?' Sierra shook her head. 'You *are* like your grandad.'

'I hope so.' Tash whirled round. 'Ta da!' She waved a sheet of folded paper at them. 'Prepare to de-code and solve the mystery of my grandad's greatest invention!'

They huddled around the strange machine and set to work. Sierra slipped a blank sheet of paper into the machine's roller. Tash sat at the machine's keyboard and punched in the letters while Elly read them out. Soon the paper was covered with words. When they had finished, Tash read them out:

Dear Natasha,

If you are reading this, it means you solved the mystery of the coding machine I left you in my will. I'm proud of you, but not surprised. You are my granddaughter, after all. It also means that you are worthy to be entrusted with the secret of my greatest invention, the coding machine you have just used.

This machine is a prototype I created for the British government. More than two dozen were made, of which this is the only one still in existence. The government did not know I had it, or it would have been taken away and destroyed along with the others. These machines were used by a secret coding centre set up and operated during World War Two in tunnels excavated beneath parts of Sunday Island. I was barely out of my teenage years, but because of my facility with codes, the government put me in charge of the coding section. I travelled secretly to and from my work via a tunnel leading from the library. I won't tell you how to find the entrance. You'll have more fun finding it yourself.

I was made to sign the Official Secrets Act and swore not to tell even my closest relatives what I was doing, so your mother knows nothing. I hope she will forgive me. As my life grew to its natural close, I found I did not want my invention to go unacknowledged by history. So I have left you the task of discovering my greatest work and keeping it safe so that future

generations will
know of the
important war
work that was
done right here
on Sunday Island.

I have left a longer account of
Sunday Island's part in the war in a
bound book in the library. I hope you
will enjoy looking for and decoding
that too!

With greatest love,
Your grandfather,
Edward Phillip Blake

Tash lowered the paper. Her eyes were bright
with tears. The only noise in the tree house
was the sound of Mojo softly snoring.

At last Tash spoke. 'He was a great inventor
after all. I hope it'll make Mum happy. I think
she always felt she had to work extra hard to

prove she could do stuff because Grandad…'
She swallowed and sniffed.

'It's weird to think of Sunday Island during a war.' Elly stared at the coding machine. 'All those people hidden in the tunnels, working away. I bet most of the islanders never even guessed. This is a really huge discovery. I bet your mum will have loads of proper historians who want to know more about your grandfather.'

'Oh!' Sierra wrapped her arms around herself and shuddered. 'You know what this means? I'm saved! I can stay on Sunday Island! Whoopee!' She leapt to her feet and whirled around the tree house, jumping over Mojo, who woke up with a strangled yip and dived for the protection of Tash's lap.

'Whoop!' Elly jumped

up and hugged Sierra. Tash joined in. Mojo began to bark with excitement.

'My dad is going to be so happy.' Sierra sighed and leant over to pet Mojo. 'Clever dog! You proved his theory. Now he can write his book and make enough money to stay on Sunday Island.'

'And now,' Tash said, 'we can go to the library and look for Grandad's book about the war and decode it. Then we can explore the tunnels and find the top secret coding centre and—'

'No way,' Sierra interrupted. 'Midnight feast first! Or I'm going to die of starvation.'

'I need food,' Elly agreed.

Tash grinned. 'OK. I'm hungry too. But I'm taking the coding machine and letter to show Mum. Grandad's not a joke any more. We have proof that his inventions work.' She slid the machine back into the puzzle box and

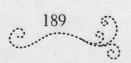

scooped them both up.

'Not the ghost detector.' Sierra grinned. 'After all this, you have to agree that there's no such thing as ghosts, Tash.'

'That reminds me,' Elly said. 'You never told us how you did the special effects in the crypt. Those were beyond amazing. How did you do the wind? And the spooky figure in white? We didn't find a projector.'

'Special effects?' Tash turned to stare at her blankly. 'I didn't. I was going to shine my torch through some plastic filters I'd cut into weird shapes, and play some spooky noises from my phone. But then I found the tunnel and...'

Her voice died away. 'You mean something happened? It wasn't me.'

Elly felt a shiver run up and down her spine. 'But that means—'

'No!' Sierra grabbed

Tash and Elly by
the hand and pulled
them to the door.
'No more spooky
stuff.' She pushed them
outside. 'There'll be time for ghosts
after a bacon sandwich and a good night's
sleep. Come on, Mojo!'

The border terrier yawned, stretched, and
pattered after them.

**Turn over for a sneaky peek
at the next book in
The Flip-Flop Club series**

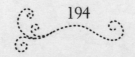

Chapter 1

'One more time, guys!' Sierra jabbed at her iPod.

Elly groaned as the *thud, thud, thud* of the electronic bass and drums started up again. Much as she loved The Sparks' hit single, *"All Together Now"*, she'd had enough. Her throat was sore with singing and her legs ached from dancing.

'Oh no you don't.' Tash staggered across the room and collapsed face down on her bed. 'You've promised "one more time" for hours now.'

'I need a break too.' Elly sank onto the

floor of Tash's bedroom. They'd cleared a big space in the middle to make a dance studio. 'My legs and brain have stopped talking to each other.'

'Come on, guys!' Sierra flicked her long dark hair over her shoulder. 'You're not trying. The singing's good but, Tash, you've got to get the dance steps sorted or we'll never win *Tomorrow's Stars!*'

Tash groaned louder. She rolled over to look at Sierra. 'It's easy for you. Dancing's your thing. I can't help it if I'm good at surfing and sailing but rubbish at dancing.'

'Tash, you're not rubbish, just tired,' Elly cut in, seeing Sierra's face grow stubborn. She 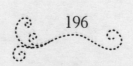 knew how much their friend wanted to win the talent contest and appear on stage at Sunday Island's music festival. But she and Tash needed a break. 'We've been practising all day, Sierra.' Elly bit back a smile as a sneaky but brilliant idea flitted into her head. 'I don't know about you, but I'm hungry.'

Sierra sniffed. 'You're not gonna get me with that one. I know I'm a greedy pig, but there are more important things than food. Well, sometimes.'

'OK.' Elly shrugged. 'I'll just have to take Aunt Dina's special spicy gingerbread cookies back home with me and tell her you didn't like them.'

Sierra's eyes grew wide. 'Gingerbread? The ones that are sort of chewy, but melt in your mouth?' Her stubborn frown faded into a dreamy look as Elly nodded. 'Where are they?'

'In my backpack.' Elly stopped trying to hide her grin.

'Training does burn up loads of calories,'

Sierra announced. 'I'll fetch the lemonade, you get the cookies.' Sierra picked up the jug of lemonade, home-made by Tash's butler, Jasper, and plonked it on the floor near Elly. 'We can talk costumes, hair, and make-up while we eat. I've brought research material,' she said and held her giant purple handbag upside down and dumped its contents. Out showered lip gloss, hair wax, sparkly headbands and hair clips, fingernail varnish in bright glittery red, purple, and pink, and half a dozen glossy magazines.

Elly lifted the plastic tub full of homemade cookies out of her backpack. She prised off the lid and a rich, warm smell of cinnamon and ginger drifted through the room. Tash groaned once more, but this time it was a happy sound. She shoved herself off the bed and padded across the floor to sit cross-legged beside them. 'I might live after all.'

Elly's stomach gave a demanding growl, then relented as she bit into a cookie. She rinsed it down with a swallow of lemonade. Delicious!

Sierra demolished three cookies, then grabbed a copy of *Music Trend* and opened to a two-page spread. **This Year's Hottest New Girl Band!** shrieked the headline.

'The Sparks!' Elly swallowed a mouthful of cookie and bent forward to get a better look. 'Wow,' she sighed. 'Don't they look totally amazing? Why can't I ever look like that?' The three members of the girl band wore sparkly jackets over their jeans and T-shirts. The jackets were embroidered to look like exploding fireworks. Marina, the guitarist, glinted in green and gold; Abi, on keyboard, sparkled silvery blue; and Lou, the drummer, dazzled in hot pink.

Sierra snorted. 'Because you haven't got a personal make-up artist and stylist. But you're right. They look great. Lou is just so cool.' Sierra pointed to the image of the tall, slender girl who sat perched at her drum kit, smiling at the camera, her long hair dyed a vivid red. 'I read that she started the drums at five and got her first gig as a drummer touring with a rock band at sixteen.'

'She's good.' Tash nodded. 'But Abi is super-talented. Keyboard holds everything together, and she does all the electronic stuff, like the bass. Plus she's a great singer. Did you know she cycled across China last year on a charity ride for disaster aid? How cool is that?'

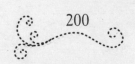

'I read about that too,' said Elly. The photo of Abi showed a petite, smiling young woman standing behind her keyboard, with her short

black hair and large dark eyes ringed with eyeliner and massive fake lashes. 'And she is really pretty. But I like Marina best.'

Elly's eyes returned to the guitarist. She wasn't as dramatic-looking as the other two band members. She was average height and had softly curling brown hair and freckles. In fact, Elly thought, she looked so nice-but-ordinary that you would hardly notice her if you saw her on the street, unless you looked into her eyes. There was something in them that grabbed your attention. 'She writes all their songs; not just the words, but the music too. And when she sings, you can see that she really means it. She's not just performing.'

'Marina is a genius,' Sierra agreed. 'But she really ought to do something with her hair. I mean, if she wasn't wearing about twenty glamour rings, a nose piercing, and those gorgeous shoes she'd look just like my RE teacher at school.'

'My RE teacher has double nose piercings *and* five tattoos,' Elly said. 'Your school needs to work on its image.'

Tash snorted, then started in surprise as the door burst open and Mojo raced into the room. The border terrier was whimpering, his tail tucked between his legs. He made a beeline for Tash and jumped into her lap with a whine.

She cuddled him in her arms. 'What is it, Mojo?' The dog whimpered more loudly. Tash lifted her head to look at Elly and Sierra. 'Something's really scared him.'

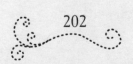

'Shhh! Listen!' Sierra cried. Her eyes turned towards the open door, a look of horror growing on her face. 'Do you hear that?'

Elly heard it now: a strange wailing cry drifted upstairs and through the door. It wavered, died, then rose to an unholy shriek.

'Oh my godfathers!' Sierra yelped, jumping to her feet. 'What is that?'

A Note from the Author

I grew up in Missouri, as far from the sea as it is possible to be in the United States. The long, hot summer holidays were spent swimming and canoeing on the lakes and rivers. My sisters, cousins and I watched crayfish wriggle along the creekbeds, waded in the streams and had our toes nibbled by swarms of minnows darting through the clear limestone waters. We snorkelled in the lakes and pretended we were diving among coral reefs and rainbow-coloured fish instead of Missouri mud and whiskery catfish. Childhood summers were full of barbecues, homemade ice cream, watermelon and twilight evenings spent catching fireflies in order to let them go and watch them spiral into the air like sparks from a bonfire.

All the time I was growing up, I longed to see the ocean and finally did on a school trip when I was the same age as Elly, Tash and Sierra. I'll never forget swimming with my friends in the sea for the first time.

Now I live in England with my family, and every summer, we spend as much time as we can on an island. My love for British islands is a big part of the joy of writing the Flip-Flop books. On my first trip to the Isles of Scilly I fell in love with the small whiskery dog of one of the boatmen: a proper seadog who trotted around the boat taking us between the islands with a cocky assurance that charmed me. I've been waiting ever since for a chance to write about Mojo! As I write, I'm taken back to some of my favourite places on earth, places very much like Sunday Island.

Ellen Richardson x

Activities
and
Quizzes

Character Profiles

Elly

Full name: Eleanor Porter

Likes: Adventures, sleepovers, films, acting, and hugs

Dislikes: Dishonesty

Favourite colour: Green

Most treasured possession: The necklace that used to belong to my mum

Tash

Full name: Natasha Blake-Reynolds

Likes: Solving mysteries, sailing, being outdoors, and animals

Dislikes: Not knowing the answer

Favourite colour: Purple

Most treasured possession: My dog, Mojo

Sierra

Full name: Sierra Cruz

Likes: The two F's – fashion and food! Especially sparkly flip-flops and Aunt Dina's cakes!

Dislikes: Ghosts and horror films

Favourite colour: Hot hot hot pink

Most treasured possession: My friends. And my purple handbag, of course!

Mojo

Full name: Mojo cute-cuddly-and-cool Blake-Reynolds

Likes: Tash, cuddles, treats, digging, and making new friends

Dislikes: Sitting still

You

Full name: _____

Likes: _____

Dislikes: _____

Favourite colour: _____

Most treasured possession: _____

Word Search

This is a word search with a twist! Once you've found all 22 words from the list, unscramble the remaining letters to spell out the name of one of the characters in the story.

G	S	P	T	S	O	H	G	M	R	*	R
*	R	T	U	N	N	E	L	O	A	E	T
H	S	A	T	I	D	E	A	J	V	T	R
O	I	N	V	E	N	T	I	O	N	*	E
S	E	C	R	E	T	*	P	*	P	T	E
I	L	*	L	O	Y	E	L	L	Y	H	H
E	R	E	U	W	E	A	S	*	*	G	O
R	*	R	T	L	M	*	R	O	L	I	U
R	M	Y	S	T	E	R	Y	D	W	N	S
A	R	*	D	E	E	W	T	C	O	D	E
O	M	A	Z	E	T	R	*	F	H	I	E
S	P	O	L	F	P	I	L	F	*	M	*

ELLY   TASH   SIERRA

GRAVEYARD   GHOST

SECRET   MOJO   CODE

FLIP FLOPS

MYSTERY

MAZE

INVENTION   LETTER

TREEHOUSE

SLEEPOVER

MIDNIGHT   TWEED

TUNNEL

HOWL

IDEA   MEET

TOUR

Character name:

_ _ _ _ _ _ _ _

_ _ _ _ _ _

Code Breaker

Break the code to reveal the secret password. Then log on to *www.the-flip-flop-club.com* and enter the password to get access to the secret section of the website!

a	=		j	=		s	=
b	=		k	=		t	=
c	=		l	=		u	=
d	=		m	=		v	=
e	=		n	=		w	=
f	=		o	=		x	=
g	=		p	=		y	=
h	=		q	=		z	=
i	=		r	=			

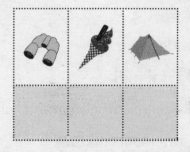

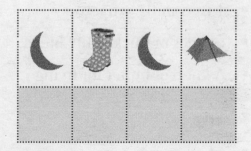

Aunt Dina's American-Style French Toast

Perfect for a special breakfast or brunch!

You will need an adult helper when it comes to frying the bread.

Ingredients

- 2 eggs
- 100g sugar
- 125ml milk
- 1 tsp ground cinnamon, plus extra for sprinkling
- 1 tsp vanilla extract
- 6 slices of thick white bread
- A knob of butter for frying

To serve

- Maple syrup
- Icing sugar

Method

1. In a medium-sized, shallow bowl, beat the eggs, then mix in the sugar, milk, cinnamon, and vanilla.

2. Cut each slice of bread in half diagonally.

3. Dip the bread in the egg mixture and leave to soak for a couple of minutes so each slice is wet through.

4. Remove the bread from the egg mixture and sprinkle a little more cinnamon over each slice.

5. Melt the butter in a frying pan, and then gently place the bread in the hot pan. Fry in batches if necessary, adding more butter as needed to stop the bread sticking. Turn the bread over so it's golden brown on both sides.

6. Serve the toast with a drizzle of maple syrup or a light dusting of icing sugar—or both!

7. *Enjoy!*

Want to join

The FLiP FLOP Club?

Find out more about Elly, Tash, Sierra, and Mojo on The Flip-Flop Club website!

www.the-flip-flop-club.com

Log on for quizzes and activities, as well as exclusive competitions and giveaways!

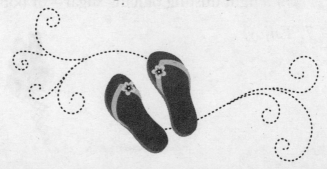